You &
The Police!

by

Boston T. Party

Illustrated by

Carroll O. Murphy

Published by

JAVELIN PRESS

c/o P.O. Box 31B, Ignacio, Colorado. (81137-0031)
(Without any 4 USC §§ 105-110 *"Federal area"* or *"State."*)
www.javelinpress.com

First Printing: *January 1996*
Printed in the united states of America,
without any 4 USC §§ 105-110 *"Federal area"* or *"State."*

12 11 10 9 8 7 6 5   / 01 00 99

www.javelinpress.com

ACKNOWLEDGMENTS

I am very grateful to Dr. Nancy Lord Johnson for her enthusiastic support of *You & The Police!*, and for her gracious Foreword.

Great thanks go to my fabulous Illustrator, the late Carrol O. Murphy for contributing on such short notice his talent and humor, which added so much flair to this book. We miss you, Cowboy Artist.

Thanks goes to K.H. for her cover layout under such time constraints.

Huge appreciation to: my editors; G.M., T.G., R.B., L.G.; and my various hosts while writing on the road; S.S., C.S., D.R., L.G., C.G., S.W, B.C., C. & S. S., M.S., A.B., and R.B.

I thank all my readers who have supported my six books, and who wrote me such nice letters. I regret that I no longer have the time to reply to them all, but I trust you'll understand how busy I've become.

Special thanks to an undeserved blessing of a lady, to whom I am infinitely indebted for her joy, humor, patient support, and unsinkable spirit--my mother.

DEDICATION

You & The Police! is dedicated to the lonely, courageous and endangered **Peace Officer**--whose battleground is sadly also within the ranks, as well as on the streets. God bless and protect you all.

Works by
Boston T. Party

Good-Bye April 15th!   (now available!)
Published November 1992. **Reprinted January 1999.** *The* untaxation classic--crystal clear and sweeping. Copied, plagiarized, and borrowed from, but never equaled. It's back, so order the *original* today!

392 pages. Now again available at long last for Ø40 + Ø5 s&h.

You & The Police!
Published January 1996. The definitive guide regarding your rights and tactics during police confrontations. Don't lose your freedom through ignorance!

128 pp. Available for Ø15 + Ø4 s&h (cash, please).

Bulletproof Privacy
How to Live Hidden, Happy, and Free!   Published January 1997. Our book will explain precisely how to lay low and be left alone by the busy-bodies, snoops, and bureaucrats. Boston shares many of his own unique methods.

160 pp. Available for Ø16 + Ø4 s&h (cash, please).

Hologram of Liberty
The Constitution's Shocking Alliance with Big Government Published August 1997. The Convention of 1787 was the most brilliant and subtle *coup d'état* in history. The federalist/nationalist framers *wanted* a strong central government, which they guaranteed through purposely ambiguous verbiage.

262 pp. Available for Ø20 + Ø4 s&h (cash, please).

Boston on Guns & Courage
Proven Tools for Chronic Problems
Published March 1998. "What if Thomas Paine had an AR-15, or if Patrick Henry went to Thunder Ranch?" A rousing how-to/*why*-to on modern gun ownership. Firearms are *"liberty's teeth"* and it's time we remembered it. Most definitive!

192 pp. Available for Ø17 + Ø4 s&h (cash, please).

Boston on Surviving Y2K*
*And Other Lovely Disasters
Published November 1998. The most thorough, in-depth, and useful guide on how to prepare yourself and your family for any disaster, natural or manmade. Covers everything from Energy to Food to Weapons to Barter, plus much more!

352 pp. Available for Ø22 + Ø4 s&h (cash, please).

a novel (yet untitled)
Due 2000. If you liked *Unintended Consequences* by John Ross and Ayn Rand's *Atlas Shrugged*, then Boston's novel will be a favorite. It dramatically outlines an innovative recipe for Liberty which neatly bypasses the bureaucracies, the courts and the Congress. (Patience! He's working on it!) ☺

TABLE OF CONTENTS

16 Our Dwindling Rights

FOREWORD

by

Nancy Lord, J.D., M.D.
1992 Libertarian Vice-Presidential Candidate

This kind of book was long overdue. Until now, only criminals and the police were knowledgeable of Constitutional rights and related case law. The law-abiding American was not.

Whatever scattered bits of *Miranda* warning trivia comprising the average American's legal understanding have been picked up undoubtedly through TV, movies and hearsay. Even those well informed are probably unaware of the practical realities when actually confronted by the police.

None of this unfamiliarity should be surprising, for seldom must law-abiding people deal with the police. Why *should* any of us be expected to know the legal requirements for a *"detention"* versus those for an arrest? Because, in Boston's words:

"Cops work for the State and the State is in search of bodies."

Government is, by definition, a legal monopoly which enjoys, also by definition, 100% "market share." Well, with an already 100% market share, the only way to grow is to increase the size of the "pie" itself. Basically, the Federal Government is increasing its "market" (those subject to regulations). **The State is *growing*.** It *needs* a quasi-moral justification for its existence. It *needs* a confiscatory tax system. **Most importantly, it *needs more* "customers"** (as Boston wryly puts it).

Government has become Business. The IRS calls its collections "revenue" (from the "Service" provided us, apparently). In Terry Gilliam's movie *Brazil*, the arrested hero was admonished by his torturers that failure to confess *"would jeopardize your credit rating."* Just so. Debt is the cheapest prison to run.

Your life, your freedoms, your productivity, and even your progeny are mere plankton for the whale of State. But to swallow you up, you must first be within its regulatory ocean. Laws by the boatload are passed every day to effect this. **More shocking yet, Government means for its laws to *be* broken--that's how people become "customers."** As Ayn Rand so presciently observed some 40 years ago in *Atlas Shrugged:*

> *Did you really think that we want those laws to be observed? ...There's no way to rule innocent men. The only power any government has is in the power to crack down on criminals.* **Well, when there aren't enough criminals, one makes them.** *One declares so many things to be a crime that it becomes impossible for men to live without breaking laws.* **Who wants a nation of law-abiding citizens? What's there in that for anyone?**

Our freedom of action is being narrowed from all sides. Pay up, shut up, and don't complain. Or *else.* We're fast becoming like Germany, where *"What's not forbidden, is obligatory."*

The old *"I Want You!"* Uncle Sam recruiting posters should today feature the federal ninja. Elderly couples are being caught in the middle of mistaken drug busts, peaceable folks lawfully owning firearms are being spitefully cleaned out by the BATF, and the routine traffic stop can now easily turn into full-blown roadside theater with drug-sniffing dogs, orange pylons and uniformed DEA agents with 9mm submachine guns. An American merely returning home from abroad is harassed by Customs officials with a swinish self-importance harrowingly similar to the now-defunct East German *GrenzPolizei.*

Extrapolate our current submissiveness a few more years hence, and national ID cards, travel permit slips, etc. are guaranteed. **But it need *not* happen.** While the State *is* powerful, it is not yet omnipotent. Some vestige of Liberty still exists, and this wonderfully unique book is about exercising it.

Instead of adding to the already weighty stack of libertarian manifestos, Boston T. Party has given us something of a refreshingly *practical* value. **Liberty is for *living*, not just knowing.** Use *You & The Police!* to live freer, while we *can.*

Nancy Lord, J.D., M.D.
December, 1995
Atlanta, Georgia

PREFACE

Let me start off by saying that *You & The Police!* is not an exhaustive legal handbook. It could not be at a mere 130 pages. It is a very comprehensive *guide* to the case law regarding your Constitutional rights vs. the powers of the police. After absorbing this book, you'll know at least as much as the cops. Such is a probably good enough for most of us.

Even still, no one book could possibly be exhaustive as case law differs amongst the 96 U.S. Districts, the 12 Appellate Circuits, and the 50 states themselves. While I can get you there 95% of the way, you'll have to do some local research to discover the finer points within your area (including your police department's policy on such things as vehicles inventories, telephonic search warrants, etc.).

So, *please* don't write me that I painted issues with too broad a brush. A broad brush is the best I could do in 130 pages. If you want to learn more, simply visit a law library. Learn how to use the West Publishing indices and how to "Shepardize" court cases. These legal issues are generally *not* terribly complex, even when interwoven, for the courts must distill their rulings to be digestible by the average cop.

Even if I *could* offer an exhaustive volume, such would become, paragraph by paragraph, slowly outdated. The law is not static, but dynamic. Though much of the case law regarding arrests, search and seizure, etc. is well established, there will always be at least *some* gradual encroachment on Liberty.

And, there is the ugly possibility of a psuedo-martial law wherein our rights are "temporarily" suspended. (I discuss this fully in the last chapter, *Our Dwindling Rights*.) If *that* occurs, all bets are off and this book will be a bitter reminder of comparatively halcyon days.

So, case law is constantly making inroads on our rights, which could be swept away entirely if H.R. 666 and its ilk passes. **My point being: we *don't* have a lot of time left to**

assert and enjoy our residual rights. At "best" they're being slowly eroded. At worst, they will be nullified by Congressional fiat. *Carpe diem!* Seize the day!

It's foolish to whine to politicians while allowing the police to bluff and bully you. In the immediate sense, this is not a political battle. Politics follow, politics react, but politics do *not* initiate. **We must win this war *individually* in real life, on the home front of our streets and cities.** Learn to assert and enjoy Liberty--while we may.

Wise up and toughen up. Get *angry.* America is fast turning into East Germany--*"Your papers!"* Get righteously indignant. We are losing our country, and not just at the macro level of national/international sellouts. We are losing America because we've grown afraid of government down to even the local level. Law abiding people are *afraid* of their police. That is *sick.* Let's get over this national wimpiness and ignorance.

This book isn't about "taking the law into our own hands." **We *are* the law!** We merely *delegate* it to the police and courts on condition of good stewardship. **Remember, the *purpose* for law is to facilitate a *reasonable* society.** The law is a *means*--not an end. The law is to serve *us*--we are not to serve the law. Let's all learn once again to be the *master.*

Boston T. Party
somewhere in America, on the road
December, 1995

Note: The Ø symbol denotes "Federal Reserve Notes" which *masquerade* as real money (backed by gold) called "dollars." Also, if I mention something without fully covering it, be patient; I'll get to it a bit further on, or in a later chapter.

- 1 -

WHO IS MY READER?

First of all, I did *not* write *You & The Police!* for career criminals. Even if I *had,* such would be largely useless to them for one of two reasons: One; being very bright, they've already developed similar techniques on their own, or Two; (and more typical) being delightfully free from the ravages of intelligence, they're too dumb to implement my ideas.

I wrote *You & The Police!* for the honest American who is being swept up in a increasingly totalitarian net.

Over the past twenty years, I have grown outraged at this snowballing Draconianism. In November 1994 I came out with a little laminated card, *Travel and the Police,* which listed in sequential order a comprehensive summary of 38 court cases regarding police confrontations. As I spoke with more and more folks on this issue, I realized they wanted more "how to" information and sample dialogue than what a 3"x10" card could provide. Thus, *You & The Police!* was born.

To my knowledge, there's no other book quite like this except for *The Outlaws Bible* by "E.X. Boozhie" (ISBN 0-915179-80-6 from Loompanics). Written in 1988, it is now a bit outdated as we've had many recent court rulings in Liberty's favor. Extremely well-researched, surprising erudite and witty, *TOB* contains much hard, real-world information from a guy who's Been-There-Done-That, including doing time in a maximum-security prison.

While our books overlap somewhat, such couldn't be avoided and is actually helpful to you, the reader. However, important differences abound. *TOB* was overtly written for the career criminal; *You & The Police!* was not. Boozhie's tone is more bitter and cynical than mine.

I discuss *TOB* because it is a fine book and the author, regardless of his crimes, deserves recognition for his ground-breaking work. I try to be scrupulously fair to authors before me, as "E.X. Boozhie." Nothing more irks me than for other "authors" to profit from my work without so much as a "howdy-do," contribute little on their own, and then portray themselves to have found the Rosetta Stone on the matter. A couple of "Boston wanna-be's" did such with my *Good-Bye April 15th!* and had to be sawn off at the knees.

If anybody out there wants to pick up where I left off and use my stuff--wonderful. But let's not have a lame rehash of something I or others have already covered in great detail. We need *new and fresh information*--not some hyper-marketed, warmed-over dish so somebody can claim to be a "cook."

WHAT MAKES *ME* AN "EXPERT?"

Though I am no criminal, I have dealt with the police often. Why? I have a "leadfoot" and have been accosted by the "Radar Brownshirts" many, *many* times. (Scores of times, actually.) My attitude towards high-speed driving is *Autobahnian.* As long as one's driving is preponderantly safe under the conditions present, what difference does the exact *speed* matter? In fact, roughly one-quarter of the states will allow you to argue this very issue in court as your right to rebut the *prima facie* presumption that exceeding the posted limits is unsafe. (I so argued in a jury trial years ago and gave the judge and prosecution a stroke! They were stunned that I knew the evidentiary rules regarding posted speed limits.)

Any arbitrary speed limit so cautious to the point of absurdity (e.g.; 55 mph limits on highways designed to handle traffic at 80+) constitutes *theft* of my Life and Property (time) and Pursuit of Happiness--*highway robbery*. Enforcement of the vile 55/65 mph limit is primarily revenue-based, and thus greedy. Hypocritical, too.

What do I mean by hypocritical? Cops routinely break the speed limit, even when they're not responding to an emergency. They even speed merely to catch up with a speeder. A fond source of amusement to me over the years has been pointing out to cops that it makes utterly no sense to *break* the same law they *enforce.* I explain that such a practice is as logical as burning down old warehouses to catch arsonists. *"What's the point of two cars wasting gas and endangering lives instead of one? I was under the impression that you were on duty to increase, not decrease, highway safety!"*

This reasoning never fails to blow a cop's mind! You've never heard such pitiful, blustery equivocation. When I promise to bring the counterproductive practice of pacing speeders to the attention of a jury, the cop often chooses to let me off with a warning! (Obviously, I don't get into any of this *unless* the cop is *absolutely* going to write me a ticket, and then I've got nothing to lose.) Anyway, tickets are written for money, not for safety. It is *true* "highway robbery."

Combined with my leadfoot and 20-40K of travel each year, I've spent dozens of hours at roadside with the police. I discuss all this so you'll know *why* I have so much non-arrest experience with the police, and thus how I presume to write authoritatively on this subject. Consider the above paragraphs a psychological and personal résumé, if you will.

I know *very* well how The Scene can go down. Also, as many of my friends are righteous cops (sworn peace officers), I get valuable inside scoop. This experience, along with my legal training, should make for a uniquely helpful book to those concerned with our growing Big Brother.

I use the term "cops" throughout mainly because most police are *not* sworn officers. An "officer" is somebody who has a *sworn* oath of office to *"support this Constitution"* (as required in VI:3). We no longer have a sworn police force. Ask your local cop if s/he swore a Constitutional oath of office. Today, cops generally work for *corporations* (cities, counties and States) as "security guards" to enforce largely corporate regulations (called *"code"*). "Police officers" would be misleading. Beyond that, I mean no disrespect by the term "cops"--that's what they call *themselves,* anyway.

Please, don't get me wrong here--I'm *not* against the police. Not as long as they behave as *sworn peace officers*. Peace officers are my friends and I would, if necessary, risk my life assisting them in their fight against violent criminals. But when truly rogue cops stomp around as "law enforcement" officers wearing black "ninja" suits and intruding upon harmless folks who in no way disturb the peace, the police no longer have my blessings.

I've been on the "front lines" in the war for Liberty for some time now, and I want to train you how to win your own battles. **How *you* handle The Scene will make *all* the difference. *You* are the most important variable, not the cop.** *You* are the one who can turn bad into good and good into bad. This book, along with some courage, will keep all but the most outrageous oppression at bay. But you must *first* be committed to exercising whatever rights are still recognized. **If you're not a *victor*, then you're a *victim*--and thus, part of the problem.**

Learn to *win*. Slough off fear. Begin *now*.

- 2 -

THE COP MINDSET

Although today's cops are better trained and equipped, their basic nature is one of humanity's constants. Deep down, the cop is a simple animal--meaning, a creature of sniff and instinct. In short, a cop is a sort of *dog.* (I mean this *metaphorically,* not pejoratively.) He relies upon his ears, nose, teeth and growl. While some enjoy the actual fighting scrape, most prefer intimidation.

THE THREE KINDS OF COPS

I can help you during confrontations with one particular kind of cop. The other two are outside my book's scope.

The Good Cop (The "GC")

is a *peace officer* and not a "law-enforcement officer." He is no zealous social reformer out to save you from yourself. Good Cop doesn't vigorously enforce unreasonable laws. He doesn't write a ton of needless speeding tickets. His attitude is, properly, *libertarian,* and will not bother those who live peaceably. He supports the 2nd Amendment and has no qualms about honest, responsible folks carrying their own firearms. He knows that his authority derives from the people and he is mindful to be a good steward of that authority. He will neither try to trick you into a flimsy "consensual" search, nor bully you into waiving your rights or offering information about yourself. Good Cop is a treasure and should be actively supported. He's nearly all alone out there.

The Rogue Cop (The "RC")

is beyond reason. Knowing the law will rarely help when he is rousting you. Then and there, you can probably only fight or surrender. Either way, it won't be pretty.

***Many*, if not most, federal agents are Rogue Cops.** Backed by tremendous resources, a vast propaganda organ, and a hierarchy willing to usurp Liberty--these hyena packs seemingly get away with anything.

They get to wear black ninja suits and masks, kick in doors without announcement, terrorize old people for hours (DEA), shove pregnant women around into miscarrying (BATF), wantonly destroy private property (IRS, etc.), stomp family pets to death (again, BATF), shoot 13 y/o boys in the back on their own property (U.S. Marshals at Ruby Ridge, Idaho), shoot mothers holding infants in the *face* with high-powered rifles, (FBI murderer Lon Horiuchi at Ruby Ridge), gun you down if you mistake them as criminal band of marauders (DEA, etc.), and flood a homestead church with hundreds of CS gas cannisters--knowing full well that the 17 children inside *did not have gas masks* (FBI at Waco). Should you be treated with such a federal visit, this book will obviously be of little help.

The Intimidating Cop (The "IC")

is, however, *is* the subject of *You & The Police!* He can still be "neutralized" on Scene with a firm, intelligent and polite stance. The State (at the *local* level) is still by-and-large Intimidating and not Rogue, as it recognizes a significant (though obviously dwindling) residual of unalienable rights.

As a personal political aside: I think that peace officers should be *drafted* into service for a brief stint of 12-18 months. **The point being: anybody who *wants* to be a cop shouldn't be *allowed* on the force.** For the same reasons that we ought to have a citizen-soldiery and a citizen-Congress, we should have a citizen-police force which rotates back into "civilian" life. "Citizen-cops" would not cultivate this "us against them" philosophy and would not likely become robotic "law enforcement officers." Tyranny seems to be historically inevitable when a nation has succumbed to a system run by career politicians, career judges, career soldiers and career cops.

WINNING AGAINST AN "IC"

Don't fight an Intimidating State (lesser measures can still work), and don't try to intimidate a Rogue State (you'll lose.)

But *how* to out-intimidate the Intimidating Cop (IC)? You *don't* do it by a growling contest, which only angers him. You see, he *believes* he's the Big Dog out there and the rest of us are puppies. He more than likely *became* a cop for its artificial power status, so he won't appreciate your challenge, which is a *personal* thing.

People are arrested for only *two* reasons: they broke the law and/or they angered the cop by transforming a generic scene into a *personal* thing. **Not creating a personal thing is paramount.** Being polite can get you off with a warning, while being a hothead jerk can get you arrested on any convenient pretext. Where no pretext exists, many IC's and most RC's will *create* such (resisting arrest, drugs "found" in your car, etc.).

The basis for intimidation is *bluff*. So, you don't try to out-bluff him, you win by subtly demonstrating that *you understand he's bluffing*. You *don't* blow up a bigger balloon than the cop's--you *deflate* his. "Blowing up a bigger balloon" (blustering about the law, or who you know, or threatening civil suits, etc.) turns the Scene into a personal matter and you absolutely *will not* win then and there, even if you're right and he's wrong. So, therein lies the trick--how to deflate his bluff balloon without overtly threatening his fragile Ego?

And now for a bit of psychology...

You want the scenario to turn into a deflated balloon in his hands, without him fully realizing when or understanding how it happened. The air simply left his balloon of bluff without a sound. It's like psyching out a snarling dog: you want him bewildered why his tough act didn't turn you into jelly. Properly done, he'll give a confused snort and back off.

It's accomplished by superior knowledge, unflappability, and dignified politeness. Not snobbery, mind you--cops hate a snob almost as much as a hothead. You want to portray an unconcerned assurance, like someone coolly taking on a winning bet. **You want to create Doubt in his mind.** I'm speaking of the Confidence of Power. Cops respect Power, and they know that there are higher powers than their gun.

Assuming that you're truly innocent of any real crime, **all the cop can do is cause you some minor inconvenience.** If he does, *and you know the law*, you can cause him some major legal headaches. You want him to understand that: ❶ You're not a criminal; and ❷ If he mistakenly treats you as one you will obtain ample legal recourse. Done well, 95+% of the IC's (and perhaps 80% of the RC's) will want you to go away.

I can teach you the basic techniques, but success requires that *you* can pull it off. Many people cannot: they're Nervous Nellies, or they're perennial hotheads, or they're devious ("hinky" in coptalk). In this confrontation only those who rightly *deserve* to will win.

The Intimidating Cop's weaknesses

His biggest weakness is that he is usually bluffing. He is standing in the air and assumes you *believe* he's on the ground. He likes standing in the air because he appears taller. He likes to appear taller than he is because his real height is below average. Not content with honest self-achievement, and reaching eye-level with the productive world, he became a cop for its exalted position of artificial authority. It's based on little more than his gun and the guns of his buddies, and deep down in his canine-like brain, he *knows it*. His gun, unlike the fully-flowered bully Rogue Cop, is more bark than bite. Intimidating Cop has neither the mature self-esteem to be Good Cop, nor the stupid testosterone to be Rogue Cop.

Intimidating Cop's weakness is his own little *self.* Inside his bluff, he's naked. You must cleverly expose his nakedness. He will then want only for you to go away. **You've made his goal coincide with your own, *and that's the idea!***

Specifically, IC is not only unsure of himself, but unsure of the *State.* Why? Because the State, the fountainhead of his supposed power, is unsure of itself. Since Americans still enjoy *some* rights and freedoms, the State must often tread lightly through a legal and procedural maze. The State is not *yet* as encompassing as Nazi Germany; it *does* have a few boundaries. These boundaries are very much in judicial flux (as are, conversely, our rights) and this makes the eager State nervous. A nervous State makes for a nervous cop, except for Rogue Cop, who is usually too far gone to be nervous.

But IC *is* nervous. He's not a lawyer. He doesn't even have a legalistic mind. So, what *does* he know about the law? Only what he's been briefed on. He was issued a legal handbook, probably compiled by the State's AG office and done in fluid three-ring notebook. New case law is handed down every month regarding stops, arrests, searches and seizures. Where do these cases come from? From IC's and RC's pushing things too far.

Your IC could be the *next* case history, and he *knows* this. But he doesn't automatically know that *you* know this. And that's *your* duty--to subtly inform him that *you* understand the dynamic boundaries, his risks and his potential costs. You want him to gradually realize that pushing a nonexistent issue with you and thereby violating your rights will gain him nothing but professional embarrassment and expense. You want him to arrive at his *own* conclusion that he'd be much better off letting you be on your way.

The IC's fears

The flip side to his insecurities is fear--that he will be found out to be small, inferior and inconsequential.

Affront to his reputation and ego.

Nothing stings an IC or RC worse than to be embarrassed by his own dumb mistake or overreaction. His Power Image amongst the public and his Status amongst peers is *everything*. Cops gossip more than old hairdressers, and to lose face is nearly intolerable. I know of a couple of great stories:

The first one comes from *Police Sniper* by Craig Roberts. Back in the 1950's and 60's when America preferred its cops as big and bright as Buicks, one such cop responded to an old lady's call about a wild animal in her basement. As a precaution against a rabid critter, Big Cop ventured downstairs with his shotgun, to discover her cat backed into a corner by a large raccoon. Big Cop blasted the raccoon. The old lady, terrified, screamed from the doorway, *"What happened?"* Big Cop told her that he had blown away the raccoon. *"Well, what about my cat?"* she asked. Big Cop shrugged and replied, *"Gee, lady--if you say so!"* and blew away her cat, too.

The second story involves a CHP who pulled over an extremely frazzled mother with a car full of kids. It was a hot summer day, the kids were howling like scalded banshees, and now she's getting this speeding ticket. Her disposition, predictably, was rather sour. The CHP, annoyed with her attitude, said something like, *"Gee, lady, what's your problem? Is it your time of the month or something?"* At that she utterly snapped and punched him out. I don't mean punched him, I mean flat knocked him *out cold*, right there on the highway!

Obviously, neither of these cops ("Whiskers" and "Kotex," presumably) will *ever* live this down!

Departmental reprimand and suspension.

A bad enough incident could jeopardize future promotions or have him reassigned into a dead end department.

Adverse media attention.

If this is sufficiently intense and unrelenting, many PD's will toss him overboard to save the overall image.

Lawsuits.

A very remote, though real, threat. Many arrested suspects swear to sue, but few actually do. Even if a damaged party is serious about suing, it requires the DA to go along, and even if *that* happens, the case takes years to reach trial.

- 3 -

PREPARING YOUR PERSON

There are two reasons to prepare your own person: 1) to avoid being detained or arrested; and 2) to avoid digging a deeper hole for yourself if you *are* frisked during a detention or searched during an arrest. *Preparation* is the key here, as you won't have the physical opportunity or cold presence of mind *during* a confrontation to improve your situation. Plan ahead for a worst case arrest scenario.

Have *no* outstanding warrants for your arrest.

I'm not talking about felonies and crimes of violence--those people *should* be arrested. What I mean are unresolved parking and traffic tickets. While it is tempting to let such slide since the cops rarely come to your door for these minor matters, *don't.* They'll surface at the very worst moments, like on the way to the airport to catch a flight. (When I was much younger, it took me a couple of times to learn this, the *hard* way.) If your freedom is important to you, then pay up and keep your *"Status Clear."* You must be able to survive a computer check, which today is quite encompassing--even nationally, if need be.

Keep incriminating stuff off your person.

This is not advice for *real* criminals guilty of *mala in se* (evil in themselves) crimes. It is intended for harmless, peaceable folk who may run afoul of various bureaucratic *mala prohibita* (wrongs prohibited).

Keep helpful information to the cops off your person.

This is trickier, as we need to carry with us the paper jumble of modern life: appointment book, credit cards, phone numbers, lists, receipts, business cards, video rental cards, discount coupons, etc. These items are obviously useful to us. They're also useful to the officials, especially if they've taken an unusually keen interest in you. Such personal and timely information speaks volumes of your habits and associations--information which would otherwise be extremely difficult to obtain. So, how to eat you cake and have it, too?

The solution which has worked well for *me* is a "palmtop" digital organizer. Roughly 3"x6"x½" and Ø100-300, it can hold quite a bit of your personal data. For example, capacity of a meager 64K means 64,000 characters. Assuming 100 characters per entry (which includes name, phone and fax numbers, address, birthdays, etc.) that's still 640 listings, which can be downloaded on your computer. Few of you will truly need more capacity, and for those who do, it's available (up to 1Meg!).

All of these palmtops offer password protection; meaning there's a public area and a secret area. Any unauthorized person trying to have a peek would be bared from the secret area. In fact, the only thing I put in the public area is a *"Cash Reward if found!"* note with a relative's phone number, so at least the unit has a chance of making it back to me if lost.

If your unit allows up to, say, 8 characters for your password, then use all 8 to increase the time and difficulty of breaking through. While I am not a computer hacker, these units seem to me fairly secure. I do not know if they are generally built with a password "backdoor," but one model of mine needed factory repair, and, as a test, I claimed to have lost my password (hoping they would admit to a "back-door"). They honestly appeared to be stumped, so I "found" my password (in order that they could save my data). If any of you have solid information of the existence of password "backdoors" on these palmtops, please let me know.

Even if your palmtop *was* taken and compromised, there is no handwriting or fingerprint evidence on the data itself, so the data may be disavowed, if you choose. Pay for the thing with cash, leave no traceable name for warranty purposes, and nobody can *prove* that you bought it, much less filled it with any particular data. If all this seems too clandestine or even "paranoid," remember (or learn firsthand) that times are serious and Liberty is quite endangered.

After you become proficient on your palmtop, you'll find that there's little need for paper notes. Any notes I *do* make on paper are mere cryptic, shorthand abbreviations. Regarding other "helpful information," for example, there's no reason to have on your person: airline tickets days before your flight, business cards and phone numbers which have already been entered in your palmtop, "to do" lists, schedules, etc.

Think of it this way: what would *your* personal papers tell the police about you if you were for some reason suddenly arrested. I posed this same question to myself many years ago after being hauled in for an old speeding ticket (which my attorney claimed to have "fixed"). Among my effects were a handwritten address book with 400+ names (this was B.P.--Before Palmtops), travel schedule, etc. All of it *could* have been easily photocopied (but wasn't) and used against me at some later date. It was a lesson I've never forgotten. Keep your personal info *private*--don't be your own enemy.

The value of "fanny packs"

What's great about fanny packs is: 1) they'll hold all your personal effects, including palmtop, pager or cell phone; and 2) they are quickly removable to lock in a briefcase or trunk. (By contrast, try discreetly emptying all your pockets while being pulled over.)

If a fanny pack does not mesh with your style, use a lockable briefcase or bag, and keep it locked in transmit. A locked container is still a fairly solid legal barrier against most general snooping. The police will need probable cause to search it.

Things *not* to have on your person:

Unlawfully carried weapons, drugs and drug paraphernalia, beepers (betokens drug dealing), phone numbers of your friends (such information should be kept in a palmtop digital organizer by Sharp, Casio, TI, Rolodex, etc. under a *memorized* password), schedules and "To-Do" lists, travel itineraries and tickets, credit cards, business cards, receipts (which locate you at a precise time and date), or more than Ø500 in cash (betokens criminal activity).

- 4 -

BEFORE GETTING
IN YOUR CAR

There are many overlapping physical preparations you should make before entering the hostile environment called *"in public."* Building on the preparations regarding your person, this chapter describes preparations you need to make regarding your car. Properly done, you'll reduce your chance of a bogus search or arrest by 95%. Trust me on this. But you must do these things *in advance*--consistently. Here they are, in rough sequential order.

Car preparations to make in advance

What I'm going to outline may seem extreme, but it's best to plan for a baseless search and/or arrest. While *You & The Police!* is for the peaceable American, you may someday become enmeshed in a nasty confrontation with the police. By protecting yourself with legal knowledge and practical preparations *before* this happens, you will hugely minimize the unpleasant outcome--possibly eliminating it altogether.

Have a locked strongbox bolted to the trunk floor.

Such proves your *"heightened expectation of privacy"* while protecting you against both car burglars and police searches gone overboard.

Army surplus stores often have sturdy, steel cases for ammo and equipment. The .50 caliber ammo cans are Ø6 and will hold a couple of pistols and ammo. The 20mm and 30mm cannon round boxes are much larger and very affordable at

Ø20. Whichever you choose, take it to a good welder for him to attach some locking hardware (or even *build* you a box). Ideally, he should construct a steel shroud surrounding the lock and hasp. The lock should be a brass Sesame or Master 4-dial combination (which eliminates the need for a vulnerable key). Use at least 3/8ths inch Grade 4 bolts with Nylok nuts and *big* washers to secure the box in your trunk or truck bed. Attach them upside-down with the bolt head underneath the floor.

What goes in your strongbox? Anything you don't want stolen, confiscated or snooped through: pistols, ammo, cash, personal papers, etc. Since a cutting torch is necessary to break in, you could affix "Flammable Materials" decals to scare off would-be torchers. The police will need probable cause (PC) to search such a strongbox.

Create a "trunk" if your car doesn't have one.

If the interior of your car is entirely open (as in vans and station wagons), its entirety is vulnerable to a *Terry* frisk since the whole *car* would probably be considered within your *"immediate control."* This is discussed fully in Chapter 7.

Small station wagons and hatchbacks often have a "privacy shelf" which rises and lowers with the rear door. If your car hasn't such a shelf, you should construct one to preclude any possibility of interior access (as with a trunk) to the rear.

Vans are more problematical. An interior wall behind the cab is required to separate the passenger compartment from the cargo area. Any door should be openable only from the back.

Take photos of your secured areas.

Photos prove, not only the structural details, but your *"heightened expectation of privacy."* This will also help disprove any false assertion that you consented to a search. Since you want the police to resort to physically breaking in such a strongbox, photos of its pristine condition are vital.

Make sure that your door locks without a key.

Many modern cars don't allow this, so to prevent the driver from negligently locking himself out. While nice for the absentminded, you do not (or *should* not) need this. As explained later, when being pulled over you'll want to be able to get out of your car and close the locking door behind you, without needing the key.

Remove the inside door panel. Operate the lock with the key to locate which connecting arm to disable. (If stumped, remove the passenger door panel to compare the internal difference. Passenger doors are lockable without the key.)

Car key preparations.

First of all, you don't want to use the original car key. You'll wear it out or break it, necessitating a replacement from the locksmith. Use your original key solely as a master to make copies--just as with software master disks. **Use copies, *not* the master!**

The copies should be utterly *generic,* without factory logos. Generic copies are not only cheaper, but if searched as a pedestrian your car keys will not immediately convey the make of your car. I do this whenever I have a rental car, for privacy, and to use the master key as a hidden spare.

Many, if not most, cars today use one key for everything: doors, glovebox, and trunk. While obviously convenient, it makes your trunk easily violated by mechanics, valet parking, and by the police. The more the cops must actually break into your property during a search, the more likely that the search will be found *"unreasonable"* and thus improper, and the more leverage you will have against them in a lawsuit. When exiting the car during a stop, your trunk key should be hidden inside the car--*not* on your person.

Buy a trunk lock and key from a salvage yard for 25-50% of the new price. Make sure that the lock is in good, operating condition and that the key fits.

Paperwork to have inside your car.

This goes beyond registration and insurance, if you're so required. If you've recently paid off a speeding ticket or, better yet, got it dismissed, keep a copy of the receipt or court disposition in your car. Computer errors abound, given the sloppy nature of traffic court personnel, and I've found it extremely helpful to be able to *prove* at roadside a bench warrant to be erroneous. While you might even still be arrested, you could later allege bad faith on the part of the cop. AAA bail bond cards are also incredibly handy to have.

Other misc. stuff to have in your car.

A radar detector is *vital* these days. Enforcement of speed limits (especially on the highways) is more for *revenue* than safety purposes. Europeans travel at 80+ mph on highways twice as congested as ours with a fourth of fatalities proportionally. Speeding tickets mean big bucks. Don't be a "winner" of this "negative lottery." Good radar detectors alerting to X, K, Ka photo radar, and laser bands can be had for under Ø100. I recommend the Uniden 2200. Mine pays for itself every month.

Have a combination lock briefcase next to you. It's roomy and secure, yet innocuous. You can disarm, legally and effectively, within seconds, as I'll describe in a few pages.

Have a microcassette with you to tape a Scene going sour. (My tape recorder has squelched two particularly bad

Scenes. The cops knew I was *serious*.) If you're *really* intent about thwarting a nasty Scene, have a camcorder and extra batteries to film a vehicle frisk or search.

Don't give the cops a single reason to stop you.

Make sure your car's plate is up to date and can withstand a computer check. Have no glaring equipment faults (broken headlight or taillight, loud exhaust, bald tires, etc.). Many criminals were *originally* pulled over for the classic broken tail or brake light. **Remember, cops work for the State and the State is in search of *bodies*.** The Scene first requires that you've drawn attention to yourself. Check out your car as a pilot checks out his airplane.

Remove political and philosophical bumper stickers, or you may offend the cop for no good purpose. (This was personally difficult for me, as I cherish a rich bumper sticker. As witty as *"If It Weren't For Guns, You'd Be A British Subject"* is, you don't want to enrage the wrong cop.) As "Chairman" Mao said, *"Move through the masses like a fish through water."* Gee, even Commies sporadically have good advice...

Your car's interior should be *clean* and nearly empty.

As the courts have said, *"The eye cannot commit a trespass."* Not only will a clean, empty interior discourage petty thievery, it offers less to the cop in *"plain view"* and reduces his time and interest at The Scene. **Check under the seats for old beer bottles or shell casings which will always roll out at the worst time.** Do not have controversial literature strewn about. Ditto for extreme forms of music. (Inside my car I have utterly no papers, letters, or books visible--a real *tabula rasa*. Very little can be gleaned about me from my car interior.) Radar detectors should be hidden as cops hate them. (Also, keep your car *clean*. If you *look* like a dirtbag, you'll be *treated* as one.) Make sure the dashboard VIN is visible.

Look like a friendly, law-abiding *"Yes, Sir!"* type.

Sprinkling about a couple of tension-reducing items is helpful: a toy or two if you have children (or better yet, a babyseat); textbooks if you're in school, etc. ***Don't*, however, overdo it!** A hint, a whiff, a mere suggestion is all you need to pass as "Joe College" or "Bob Family Man." On this note, *"Say No To Drugs"* and *"Sheriff's Association Member"* stickers are too overt and often make the cop suspect that you're trying too hard to *appear* law-abiding. As I said, don't overdo it. Cops are good at detecting the *too* obvious. Too much of a "white flag" can easily be a "red flag"--know what I mean?

Have no drugs or residue in your car/on your person.

Obviously.   Life is greatly simplified when drugs are absent. This is especially true regarding You and the State.

The federal courts have held (mistakenly, in my view) that a dog sniff doesn't first require *"probable cause"* (PC) because such isn't technically a *"search"* under the 4th Amendment. Well, *that's* neat. The *"plain smell"* doctrine applies also to dogs, and their alerting to drugs creates PC. (Some states may, happily, have more restrictive rules on dog sniffs.)

In *my* view, anything beyond a human's senses is a *"search."* Whenever a cop's 5 senses are amplified through the use of *any tool* (binoculars, parabolic microphone, X-ray, a dog's nose, etc.), such, to me, is a *"search"* within the meaning of the 4th. But that's *me*.

So, the police were provided with a neat loophole--the drug-sniffing dog. From my understanding, the dog is tough to beat. If you are carrying drugs, and the cop is suspicious enough to call for a dog, you *will* be sniffed and found out. Those who smoke pot regularly will carry enough smell on their body and clothes to alert a dog, even if they've no pot in their car (or *your* car). Bummer, dude.

Worse yet, even if you've never used drugs, the dog will likely alert to the smell left behind by a passenger, mechanic or former owner of your car. Therefore, if you buy a used car, have it *thoroughly* steamcleaned and deodorized.   Check in seatcracks, and underneath the seats for an old "roach." Threaten to horsewhip anyone who brings so much as drug *residue* into your car.

If you have friends who use illegal drugs, explain the foolish risks to you. If you're in *their* home or car, you'll probably pick up enough of a residue to later alert a drug dog, so be careful. Also, you might be there if *they* get busted. If so, you *will* be detained and frisked--maybe even arrested and searched.

Lock ALL other items in the trunk.

If you don't *absolutely* need it on the road, stow it in the trunk. Contents in your trunk are not within your *"immediate control"* are immune from a *Terry* frisk and *"search incident to arrest."* (Full-blown PC is necessary to search there, unless your car is impounded and treated to an *"inventory search."*)

If not carried on/about your person, firearms should not only be unloaded and in the trunk--but in a locked container. Ditto for personal papers. That way, in case an IC gets in your trunk he is then thwarted by additional locked containers. (I read about a druggy who had a small *safe* in his trunk. Upon arrest, the cops seized his safe (for "inventory purposes") but couldn't crack it before the druggy was sprung. Druggy got back his unopened safe. Sometimes even dirtbags have some clever moves. I say: Learn where and when you can. Or, everybody *else's* stuff is grist for *my* mill.)

Totally benign items such as shopping bags, etc. should also be stored in the trunk. Reason being, such is *information*. If the local SEARS was just robbed and the bandit escaped in a car similar to yours, the cop who is now writing you a speeding ticket might think he's actually busted the creep because of the SEARS bag on the seat. Far fetched? Yeah, probably--however, I wouldn't take *any* chances. **You want to give the cop *nowhere* to go.** Keep your car a real *tabula rasa* which connotes/implies *nothing*. It could be a vital edge...

Have a way to secure a personally carried firearm.

In open-carry holster states, I do so and exit the car wearing my pistol if stopped. Such is perfectly lawful. I do not swagger or bluster because of my pistol--in fact, I act as if it doesn't exist. If he brings it up, I stress that *I'm on his side*, that I take gun bearing very seriously and do *not* carry to intimidate the public. Interestingly, in the three times I've been stopped in open-carry states for speeding, I was *always* let off with a polite warning. (One Good Cop engaged me in pleasant conversation and actually gave me a mini *salute* when we parted!) My impression over the years is that *most* (though not all) cops respect the courteously armed.

Most states, however, do *not* honor the 2nd Amendment and prohibit the open carry of firearms. Concealed carry, if allowed at all, is by permit only. So, what to do if pulled over in a non-open carry state? You must have a quick, subtle and foolproof way to unload and lock away your gun *while being pulled over*. **Quick**--less than 15 seconds. **Subtle**--with almost no obvious body movement. **Foolproof** against a *Terry* frisk, *"search incident to arrest"* and *"inventory search."*

I recommend a combination lock briefcase, left open on the passenger seat or floor. When being pulled over, quickly and discreetly unload your gun, lock the ammo in the glovebox or some *closed* container (the ammo must be *separate* from the gun and mag, and *not* in the same container), put the gun in the case, close and spin the dials. Your gun is neither loaded nor *"on or about the person"* and therefore you are no longer armed by general legal definition. In this condition, if asked if you have a gun in the car, say "No." Even if they found out, you couldn't be prosecuted for not admitting that you had a gun.

Or, quicker still, travel with your gun in the case un-locked. You'll be able to draw it quickly, or secure it quickly, de-pending on the situation. If time is too short, I would simply toss the gun, still loaded, in the case and lock it. That's at least better than nothing, and the cops wouldn't know it was even in there, much less loaded, unless they broke into your case.

Don't practice locking up during the Scene--you'll be too nervous to do it well. *Practice this* with a friend watching from behind your car. You must be able to do this smoothly, or else the cop will get suspicious.

Even if the cops illegally break in your briefcase, carrying a locked, unloaded gun generally *isn't* unlawful (except in N.Y.C., D.C. and some Eastern states)--meaning the cops will illegally come up with zip (unless your gun was listed in the Na-tional Crime Index Computer (NCIC) as once stolen--so check it before buying).

Have *only* these essentials on your person.

If pulled over, the only things to have on you are:

> license/registration (or the Sovereign equivalents),
> AAA bond card, or sufficient bail cash for any likely fine,
> some pocket change to make phone calls,
> microcassette recorder,
> your lawyer's card, and
> a second car door key hidden on you.

Your other keys should be on separate, detachable ring and hidden. (If asked to open you trunk, refuse or reply that you misplaced the key.) *Only* these things do you need then, and *only* those things should you have on you. Everything else should be locked in a briefcase, and/or locked in the trunk.

Some final thoughts on preparation

This sums up the physical preparations you *should* have made and practiced *before* The Scene. I fully realize that the totality of these preparations seems rather extreme, but *without* such The Scene itself can *easily* become extreme--especially if you reserve your rights, refuse consent of a search, etc. **Trust me on this. It's the sum of the *little things* which count.** It's the *little things* which separate the amateur from the professional, the victim from the victor. **Remember, *all the mistakes have already been made*--so why do any of us need to reinvent the square wheel?**

I've watched countless episodes of *Cops* and the like, read hundreds of crime novels and legal cases, all the while asking myself, *"How did this guy blow it? Where was he his own enemy? When did the cops bluff because of the guy's ignorance?"*

Once detained (or worse, arrested) you will *not* have much (if any) freedom to physically better your situation. You must play the cards you dealt yourself *before* the red lights flashed. Think of the above as insurance. Buy it now for later. The rest is mental preparation, a bit of confidence, and experience.

In short, don't draw attention to yourself.

Do not travel at outrageous speeds or flagrantly disregard safety laws. Wear your seat belt. (Yeah, I know it's hilarious fun to drive 95 mph, drinking a beer, steering with your feet, and throwing trash out the sunroof while shooting at road signs--but *cool* it!) Remember, if it's rude, it's probably illegal. **Look and act like prosperous, law-abiding middle-class!**

About speeding, at some point such is automatically considered to be *"reckless driving"*--usually 25mph or more in excess of the posted limit (states vary on this) and is at least a full-blown misdemeanor. If you travel a fast clip, be aware of when *"reckless driving"* kicks in.

A last bit of advice

Take care that these preparations as a visual whole do not ironically attract attention. (Such a warning was the moral of the armored car cartoon.) In a conversation with Nancy Lord, she expressed concern that the strongbox was a tad much and would make the cops suspicious. She has a point. You *don't* want such precautions to be obvious, or even visible--so have the strongbox in the trunk, not on the back floor. (The only way they'd know it was in the trunk is via a PC-based search, or an impound inventory search. Either should be very rare for my intended readers.)

Therefore, do what is *reasonable* in your situation. Think your strategy through, be coolheaded and deliberate. Don't get all freaked out. It is highly unlikely that anyone is out to get *you* personally. Just don't draw attention by being *too* clever.

- 5 -

NEVER CONSENT!

This will be the shortest and, ironically, the most important chapter of *You & The Police!*

Many folks I spoke with expressed no small surprise at my recommended firm posture with the police. As you might have already gathered, I do not advise *any* sort of kowtowing or compromising during The Scene.

"But you were the one who needlessly aggravated the whole deal!" many remarked after hearing my "war stories." Assuming a short-term perspective to be paramount, they're right--my intransigence *did* cost me time and inconvenience. For *me,* however, the mere momentary convenience is rarely paramount. In confrontations with the police I take the *long* view, and I think *you* should, too.

During The Scene, cops rely upon the public's overwhelming desire to have the confrontation end. Most people will, in the hope of speeding up a cop's exodus, divulge, consent, placate, whatever--*anything* to make him go away. While this wimpy expediency will *usually* work to that effect, you may instead further confirm the cop's suspicions, or even give him probable cause to arrest you.

For example: By voluntarily surrendering ID during a mere contact, he could discover some unpaid ticket and warrant for your arrest. By offering your prior whereabouts you could unknowingly place yourself at the scene of some crime. By admitting association with certain persons you could drop yourself into their legal mess. One never knows.

I've said this before, and I'll say it again: **Cops work for the State and the State is in search of *bodies!*** The police exist to arrest criminals. During *any* confrontation with the police, there is at least *some* risk that *you* could be arrested. Remember, they wouldn't be talking to *you* in the first place unless *you* were somehow a potential "customer."

Remember, fish are caught only because they opened their mouths! Keep yours *shut!*

I'm not saying that cops are always, or even generally, our adversaries, but they *can* be during any Scene. It's one thing to assist the police in catching criminals by giving information, **but *watch out* when they start asking about *your* activities.** My rule is not to discuss with officials anything related to myself. I do not answer personal questions, **and I *never* consent to a requested search of my property.**

If a cop asks to search your property, all sorts of warning bells should go off. Understand this: **There is *never* any real advantage to a consented search. Always, always, *always* refuse consent.** I don't mean often, or usually--I mean *always!* If you learn nothing else but *this* from my book, you'll probably fare well.

"Well, I can get a warrant!" the cop may menacingly retort. You should reply, *"I doubt it. Warrants are based on probable cause, and since I haven't done anything wrong there can be no probable cause of any crime. Nice try, but save it for some dirtbag--preferably an ignorant one. Good day, Officer."* Walk away, close the door--shut down The Scene. (I'll show you exactly how in Chapters 6, 7, and 8.)

- 6 -

THE CONTACT

There are three kinds of scenarios between you and the police: *contact/encounter, stop/detention, and arrest/custody.* Listed in order of severity, they require increasing amounts of crime-related evidence to be upheld. More is required to detain than to contact, more to arrest than to detain, and more to convict than to arrest.

Evidence vs. Arrest Triangle

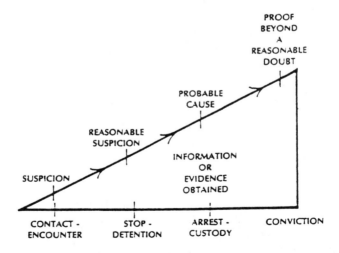

The object of my book is to teach you to recognize this progression of lawful restraint and how to "nip in the bud" any police confrontation you might have *at the lowest level possible.*

The information required to do so increases at each successive stage, as do the risks. I could *give* away the mere pamphlet needed for the contact stage, like on changing the oil in your car.

However, for you to defuse the next stage (detention) requires *much* more information. This would be like giving your car a full tune-up. Arrests I'll leave for Chapter 9.

THE CONTACT / ENCOUNTER

This is simple consensual conversation between a cop and a private individual who can walk away or ignore the cop's questions. **While this seems innocent enough, always remember that cops are *never* truly "off duty."** I don't have a general problem with that, as criminals are never truly "off duty," either. Happily, most criminals are astoundingly stupid liars. Well knowing this, cops can make effortless small talk with suspects to uncover *"probable cause."*

It's amazing what cops discover simply by asking. Thank God that criminals are generally morons. A retired California deputy told me about a kid on a bicycle with bulging pockets. Making simple contact, he asked, *"Hey, what's in your pockets?"* Instead of brushing off the question, the kid replied, *"My stash!"* *"Really, wow! Can I see?"* The little genius then pulled out ounces and ounces of pot. The moral: to the cop it never hurts to ask, and it's never illegal, either.

Legal basis for the contact / encounter

No suspicion is required for a cop to merely contact you.

> *There is nothing in the constitution which prevents a policeman from addressing questions to anyone on the streets.*
> *-- Terry v. Ohio.,* 392 US 1 (1968); concurring opinion

Also, contacts made during a cop's "caretaking" capacity:

> *...arise from the police officer's duty to maintain peace and security, to protect citizens from harm or annoyance and to do all those innumerable tasks which society calls upon police to do.*
> *-- Batts v. Superior Court,* 100 Cal. Rptr. 181 (1972)

The above case arose when a cop knocked on a van door late at night to warn the occupants inside about the town's ordinance against sleeping in cars. Batts (rocket scientist in a former life) opened the van door exposing a pot party in progress, complete with pipe and weed in plain view. Such evidence was admissible, as no detention had occurred (which *would* have required *"reasonable articulable suspicion"*). Learn from Mr. Batts. Waving contraband around in front of a cop even when he's doing you a favor is...an *error*. Gee.

Your rights during a contact

Nearly total. You have the utter right to ignore him and walk away. Simple. **You are not required to tell him your name, much less provide ID.**

The cop's powers during a contact

Nearly zero. If you disengage, there's *nothing* he can do without the required *"reasonable articulable suspicion"* for detention or *"probable cause"* for arrest. He can, however, walk along with you in public and observe.

He *does* have the right and the power, during *any* kind of confrontation with you, to frisk you for weapons *if* : he has a reasonable belief that you are armed *and* that you pose a threat to him or the public. **He cannot *routinely* frisk *everyone* he contacts, or even detains.** He must first have reasonable belief of a threat based on articulable facts (***Terry v. Ohio,*** 392 US 1 (1968)). The so-called *Terry* frisk is limited to the patting down of clothing for weapons. He cannot reach into pockets for objects clearly not weapons.

He can most likely prohibit you from having your hands in your pockets (***People v. Ross,*** 265 Cal.Rptr. 921 (1990)). As a legal rule of thumb, the cop's *"reasonable"* perception of his safety will nearly always override your Constitutional rights.

The realities during a contact

Don't *believe* he's only being friendly--it's a fishing expedition. **Cops chat up people like guys chat up chicks.** We're talking ulterior motive, here. Don't be like some buxom, yet naïve, 17 y/o girl. He's not interested in your love of grandma and puppy dogs.

I've conversed with many cops. As I am a clean-cut, lawful type, I rarely tweak their antennae, so our talks have usually been benign and friendly. *Usually*. When they weren't, and I knew much less, I still managed to avoid any real hassle because of my innocence and innate righteousness indignation. This was a crutch until I became more wise to The Scene and how to defuse it. Today, however, there is no time for you to learn all this the *slow* way. You need this crash course.

Practical tips during a contact

If a cop shows enough interest in you to make contact, it's very likely he has a hunch that you're up to something. **You have only two goals at this stage:** First, not to give him anything more than he *believes* he already has, and second, to leave his presence. *Nothing good* can come from you hanging around. Leave and get out of sight.

By *voluntarily* talking you might somehow give the cop grounds for detention or arrest--*even though you're completely innocent of any crime!* I can't emphasize this strongly enough. I fully realize that this goes against the peculiarly American grain of innocent openness, but you absolutely must learn when and how to *shut up!* You could, unwittingly, admit to having been at/near a crime scene, or knowing somebody criminally implicated. You could even "confess" to something you had no idea *was* a crime.

There is *no* advantage to answering questions about yourself during a contact. *Ever.* The *only* place to defend yourself is in a jury trial. Let the State drag you there *without your help*. **Offer/answer nothing--ever!** Even though he can *ask* you anything, you do *not* have to answer. You can simply ignore him, or reply something like:

> *"I don't have time to talk right now. Good day."* or,
> *"Sorry, but if I'm late again, it's my job!"* or,
> *"I can't believe you'd ask such a personal question!,"* or
> *"I was brought up not to talk to strangers."* or even,
> *"My consulting fee is Ø50 per minute, with a two minute minimum. Do you accept?"*

and walk away, as from any airport Moonie. Almost any kind of departure will work here. Just keep it short and sweet.

If unlawfully carrying a weapon during a contact.

You're at a severe disadvantage if on foot. In a car you have ample time and means to secure a weapon (as thoroughly explained in Chapter 4), but *not* as a pedestrian. So, be careful how/when you carry in public, *especially* in states which have no conceal carry provision. Cops are good at discerning concealed weapons--their lives *depend* on it. Pistol fanny packs are well known, at least in big cities. Shoulder holsters are fairly conspicuous. Inside the pants under a heavy shirt, vest, or jacket is best. **Don't do so unless you are 100% discreet.**

Avoid making contact with the police if you're carrying unlawfully. Don't make eye contact, smoothly change directions and glide away. Should a contact be unavoidable, leaving is still your top priority, even if only to round a corner and ditch your weapon temporarily. The courts will justify almost *any* preemptive frisk for weapons as the cop's legal right, so you don't want to prolong a contact until he suddenly decides on a *Terry* frisk.

Stay calm and cool!

Overall, this is the important thing: *do not act nervous.* Nervousness, combined with other variables *might* be enough to create reasonable suspicion in the cop's mind. Do not keep looking back, do not run, do not begin rearranging your stuff, do not head directly for a phone. In other words, don't freak out. Just get out.

Personally, my exodus is not usually so abrupt as I often talk to him a bit to discover why he's sniffing about, *and* to keep up my edge. (I don't recommend such for the beginner, obviously. Stay squeaky-clean and you won't *need* an edge for the detention stage.) With all my experience at this, even *I* don't needlessly stretch out a contact. This can be a high stakes dialogue, and you might have a really clever cop who wheedles something damaging from you.

When to increase your wariness.

If the cop for some reason *does* become suspicious of you, it takes keen experience to sense the subtle shift. **"Friendly**

Cop" can slide into Suspicious Cop without missing a beat. (The *eyes* are the giveaway; they'll become tighter and more focussed. This is why cops often wear sunglasses.) Be polite, but remain coolly wary. **Cops work for the State, and the State is in search of *bodies*.** When his eyes tighten and his questions become slightly more personal--*beware*.

The pedestrian advantage.

Oh, one last thing. Most contacts are pedestrian, versus detentions/arrests on the road (where you've *already* been stopped for some infraction). I would *not*, therefore, return directly to your car, especially if the contact was rather eerie or inexplicable. A clever IC or RC can concoct a dozen excuses to detain or even arrest you on the road ("speeding," "rolling through a stop sign," "failure to signal," etc.), while detention or arrest is much more difficult when you're just walking down the street. Indirectly return to your car without him seeing.

Once, I *did* experience a mere contact with police on the road. I had stopped to free a sticking choke and a highway patrolman pulled over behind me a minute later. I was lawfully wearing my pistol in plain view. Instead of letting *him* get out and initiate The Scene, I walked back, explained my problem through his window, thanked him for his concern, and returned to my car--not letting him say a *word!* He sat there, stunned, for about 20 seconds. I never looked back at him. He then drove away. Being polite and taking charge goes a long way.

- 7 -

THE DETENTION

This not an arrest, but an *"intermediate level of intrusion"* which is a brief and so-called *"reasonable"* suspension of your freedom until the cop can uncover the required *"probable cause"* for arrest. You're not under arrest, but you're not free to go, either. As ruled in **Adams v. Williams,** 407 US 143 (1972):

> *The Fourth Amendment does not require a policeman who lacks the precise level of information for probable cause to simply shrug his shoulders and allow a crime to occur or a criminal to escape. On the contrary...it may be the essence of good police work to* [detain the suspect to ascertain his motives and question his behavior].

If you are lawfully detained, it's probably because you made yourself conspicuous and stupidly attracted attention.

Legal basis for detentions

A detention/*stop must* be based on *"reasonable articulable suspicion"* **(RAS) that you were/are involved in some criminal activity.** RAS is more than a mere hunch. It is the combination of several *facts* which a reasonable officer would conclude as articulable suspicion, such as:

❶ Concealment
❷ Flight at sight of officers
❸ Unusual movements
❹ Abandonment of property
❺ "Casing" a place
❻ Checking back and forth as a "look out" man would
❼ Disguises
❽ Presence at scene of a crime
❾ Information from a reliable informant

Usually, though not always, the courts require more than one of the above as a *pattern* of conduct. Merely being out late at night and briefly peering through a store window, by example, would probably not be enough to create RAS. Going *back* to the store and acting furtively probably *would* create RAS. Clearly, there are no hard rules here, so beware. A good rule of thumb is: don't behave so suspiciously that *you'd* phone the police on somebody *else* emulating your conduct. Examples of a cop's experience-based information are:

- ❶ High crime area
- ❷ Suspect does not "fit" in neighborhood
- ❸ Suspect is a known addict, burglar, etc.
- ❹ Manner of packaging (especially drugs)
- ❺ Smells (e.g., marijuana)
- ❻ Association with known criminals

The cop's powers during a detention

If you do not stop, or attempt to leave, the cop may restrain you in a manner reasonable when considered in light of the purpose. If you try to flee or struggle, the cop may even cuff you, especially if you are suspected of a violent crime. However, if the cop handcuffs a compliant detainee in a non-emergency, the *"seizure" will* be considered an arrest by the court.

Some areas may *try* to require you to provide ID during a lawful detention (check this out in your state and federal judicial district), though these laws are generally held to be unconstitutional (***Brown v. Texas***, 443 US 47 (1979)). No *"Miranda"* warning is required here, so *you* must be aware of your rights because the cop will not inform you *until* an arrest.

You may be *Terry* frisked for weapons only if the cop has a good faith belief that you might be armed *and he has a particular fear of his safety*. The frisk is limited to patting you down.

He may bring eyewitnesses to the scene for an immediate confrontation. He may conduct a limited investigation of crimes (e.g.; to determine if nearby homes have been burglarized when detainee is suspected of such).

How long can he hold a detainee?

The cop generally has up to 20-30 minutes to find *"probable cause"* for an arrest, or you're free to go. While the courts have not and cannot set a rigid time limit, 90 minutes is *definitely* too long, 60 minutes *probably* is, and 45 minutes is a legal coin toss. What is *"reasonable"* depends on the circumstances, the officer's degree of diligence and his use of the least intrusive means to confirm his suspicions. He cannot drag his feet trying to buy time.

If, however, you've landed at JFK and the feds have RAS that you're a "swallower" (somebody who smuggles heroin or cocaine in swallowed condoms), all rationality goes out the window. In *U.S. v. Odofin,* 929 F.2d 56 (2nd Cir. 1991), a Nigerian landed at JFK and was detained as a swallower. He refused to submit to an X-ray or intake laxatives, so the feds held him until he passed his stomach contents. Normally this happens within 48 hours, but Odofin was committed to waiting them out. He withheld for *24 days* and his detention was *upheld!* The court "reasoned" that Odofin himself was responsible for the length of his detention since he didn't submit to radiation or laxatives.

Your rights during a detention

For you, my law-abiding, informed reader, I'd say it's about 70/30, favoring you. (For the ignorant sap--usually a criminal--it drops to 10/90.) You are *not* free to walk away, though you may *not* be forcibly moved to a squad car or the police station as such constitutes an arrest.

While the cop is not required to *"Mirandize"* you here, you still do *not* have to answer questions or ID yourself. The legal rationale for the intermediate level of intrusion of the detention is that *answers are consensual.*

> *...The defendants' refusal to furnish identification--***which they were entitled to do...*[in] *a* **Terry** *stop...*
>   *-- U.S. v. Brown,* 731 F.2d 1491, at 1494 (1984)

> *We must emphasize that* **we do** **not** **hold that a suspect may be detained and searched merely because he either refused to identify himself or refused to produce proof of indentification.**
>   *People v. Loudermilk,* 241 Cal.Rptr. 208 (1987)

> *...[T]he detainee is not obliged to respond.*
>   *-- U.S. v. Rokowski,* 714 F.Supp 1324 (1987)

Though you do *not* have to answer questions of give ID, failure to do so will tend to raise, not dispel, the cop's suspicions. He will then be justified in giving you a *Terry* frisk. All this means is that the detention will last a bit longer. Big deal. He won't like your reticence. Big deal. Your goal is avoid being arrested, and if silence is the surest route, then so be it. What he's looking for is probable cause, or something which *leads* to PC.

If PC doesn't exist, then you're free after a few minutes (unless he *concocts* PC, which *is* a possibility). Even if PC *does* exist, you're free if he can't find it before the clock runs out. Time is on *your* side. Also, to my understanding, you have the right to demand that he express his RAS to you.

Will this happen to *me?*

Assuming you've prepared yourself as described, the chances of a detention are slim. As I mentioned in Chapter 4, cops *rarely* roust a clean-cut, law-abiding type. Also, they show remarkable restraint in rousting the scruffier types. On the whole, whenever *I've* been detained, the cops had a valid reason by legal standards. Of my approximately 150 detentions, I was legitimately stopped about 90% of the time (usually for "speeding," etc.). Only 10-15 times was I ever originally stopped for basically no reason or, worse yet, some truly concocted pretext.

So, if you're detained, the odds are that you've done something to give the cop RAS (e.g.; a "traffic" offense, or that you're unlawfully concealing a weapon). The *next* most likely reason is that by innocently being at the wrong place at the wrong time, you've unawaredly immersed yourself in an investigation (odds are 10%). (The family dog *can* be caught in a wolf trap.) This has happened to me several times, and I didn't understand why until they had asked a few illuminating questions. Finally, the *least* likely scenario is that you're simply being rousted *without* legal cause (a 5% likelihood).

If you don't give the cops cause for attention, the only way to be detained is by unaware proximity/association with a crime, or textbook rousting. Either are pretty rare.

Practical tips during a detention

A mere contact can easily and subtly ripen into a detention. If you feel increasing not at liberty to leave, the situation has probably sunk to a detention. Although cops are allegedly instructed to reassure the contact of his freedom to go, as well as announce when the situation has ripened into a detention, they are *rarely* this candid. Once, when an RC was rousting me for my lawfully holstered pistol, I had to demand *three* times if I was being detained! When he realized that his bullying tactics did not make me wet my pants, he retreated, gave me his little lecture and stomped off.

There is a simple way to clarify The Scene--**you should express a *firm, clear* desire to leave and ask him if you are free to go.** Don't respond to questions or demands *until* he's answered this. If you are being detained, he *must* admit it. Be polite, but firm, and keep him in his place. *He's* bound by more case law and procedure than you--never let him forget it.

Handling The Scene when the cop has RAS.

The cop's questions *must* relate to the purpose of the stop (his RAS), or else the detention is unreasonable. That's why you should *first* pry from him his RAS so that you can keep his questioning within proper bounds.

Cop: *"No, you are not free to go, and yes, I'm detaining you. You've walked up and down this block three times in the past hour, looking around like you're casing the area. I've never seen you before around here, and your actions were suspicious to me.*

You: *"Oh, I see! A friend told me to meet her at a store to help pick out a gift, but I forgot the name. I was hoping to run into her or maybe remember the store by walking around, and was about to call her when you came up to me.*

Your response is perfectly believable and should at once allay his suspicion. A reasonable explanation *should* spring you. Some cops, however, will probe a bit further:

Cop: *"How were you planning to call her if she's by now at some store you don't even know the name of?"*

You: *"Well, fortunately she carries her cell phone in her purse."*

At this point, by the cop's probe of your story, you should be *quite* on guard. I would quickly and smoothly change the tenor of the situation by offering, *"Hey, I can call her from this pay phone to find out where she's at and then you can tell me how to get to the store. I'd really appreciate that! She's probably wondering by now what happened to me."* By taking charge you've changed the dynamics and totally deflated The Scene. First, you proved your story was true and then "demoted" him into a mere directions-giver. There's little way he could refuse.

When you're innocently caught up in another's crime.

Let's say you're out jogging late at night. A house is hit a few streets over by a burglar in a dark running suit, though you're unaware of this. A cop spots you, has RAS because your proximity and resemblance to the burglar, pulls over and tells you to stop. Any reasonable person would conclude that he is not free to go, and his state of mind is the legal basis for determining detention vs. mere contact.

You must be *very* careful here. Even though you are utterly innocent of the burglary, there is a significant chance that you might be arrested and even convicted.

Cop: (Politely, though firmly:) *"Evening, Sir. May I see some ID?"*
You: (Absolutely calm:) *"I don't usually carry it with me when I'm just out jogging. My name is _____, and I live over on Maple Street. What's this all about, Officer? Have I done something wrong?"*

Here, you've accomplished several important things: ❶ You've explained why you don't have ID (assuming one must produce ID during a lawful detention in your state or judicial district); ❷ You've pleasantly identified yourself nonetheless; ❸ You've explained your activities to be benign; and ❹ Having satisfyied the cop's basic questions, you've asked him his reason for stopping you--his RAS. The ball is now in his court.

If he replies in an appeased tone that there was a burglary on Pine St. and he was checking out anybody matching the burglar's description, then you're probably home free. However, if he persists in a suspicious tone, beware:

Cop: (Not satisfied:) *"Were you on Pine St. a few minutes ago?"*

Your alarm bells should *really* be going off now! He is still fairly convinced that you're the burglar. Your goal at this crucial point is to stand firm and not give the cop *anything* to allow an extended detention or a possible arrest.

If you *do* admit to having been on Pine St., he will then have cause to detain you further until the homeowner is brought to identify you. If you are unlucky enough to have the same general height, build and appearance of the burglar--and the conditions were poor enough--there's a good chance of being erroneously fingered.

You: (Reasonably:)   *"Look, I haven't done anything wrong. Did something just happen over on Pine St.?"*
Cop: (Intensely:)   *"Just answer me--were you on Pine tonight?"*
You: (Polite, though a bit more firm:)   *"Now, officer, this is concerning me. I mean, put yourself in my shoes. You're out jogging, minding your own business, get suddenly pulled over and asked your whereabouts earlier. I haven't done anything wrong, and I don't know of any crimes just committed on Pine St.--or else I would have already phoned in. Now, I think I have a right to know what's going on here, don't you?"*

By *not* jumping into any legal arguments/demands and retaining a common-sense "I-haven't-done-anything-wrong" position, you have kept The Scene mature and reasonable. The cop should realize that you're just an innocent jogger, soften up and explain. However, if you've got an IC or RC, it gets tougher:

Cop: (Now getting angry:)   *"No, you don't 'have the right to know what's going on here'! You need to start answering my questions! Were you on Pine St. a few minutes ago?"*

If you *were* on Pine St.--do *not* lie. I understand it would be tempting to deny it and get the cop out of your face, but it can easily come back to bite you later. For example, it's possible that somebody either saw you there or can say that you regularly jog on Pine--and either will impeach the *rest* of your story, which is truthful. To succeed through lying requires: ❶ the cop to *believe* it, and ❷ *nobody* (including *yourself* through stupidity or forgetfulness) disputing it later. These are *not* reliable odds. Besides, since you are *not compelled* to answer, there's no reason to lie about it. Handle it like this:

You: (Not rising to his anger, though quite firm:)   *"Officer, I don't want this to get out of hand here. I understand that you're trying to do your job and apparently something just happened on Pine St. Whatever happened there I had no part in and whoever did is getting away right now. I'm trying to help you here, but I don't know anything about any crimes committed. This is all I have to say and I'd like to be on my way right now. **Am I free to go?**"*

The above volunteers nothing even indirectly damaging, restates with firmness your innocence and forces the cop to decide whether he can detain you further. The most he can do is bring the homeowner over to look you over. **As I said, this is a *highly* dangerous predicament.** I would protest such as extremely prejudicial against you as the recently burglarized homeowner is likely to be quite emotional and intent on finding the thief. This state of mind, and the unavoidably incriminating fact that the cop *already* has you detained as a suspect, clearly *begs* for a classic misidentification. I would further insist that a formal lineup is the only way to be fair, especially sinces there's no evidence of your being on Pine.

Handling yourself during a roust

You will *someday* be "rousted" and how *you* handle it is more important than the roust itself. Be polite, yet firm:

Cop: (Matter-of-factly:) *"What's in your bag?"*

You: (Breezily:) *"Lawful private property. I'm surprised you'd ask such a personal question! Sorry, but I've things to do--**am I free to go?***

Cop: (Mildly sarcastic:)   *"Well, if it's 'lawful private property' then there's no reason to mind if I had a look, is there?"*

You: (Coolly indignant:) *"As a matter of fact, I would mind. It's a waste of my time as a law-abiding Citizen and a waste of your time as a peace officer in search of criminals. As I said, I've got a rather busy day and must be on my way. **Am I free to go, or are you detaining me?***

Cop: (Sternly:) *"You mean you won't let me look in your bag?"*

You: (Firmly:) *"That's right. **I wish to leave now--am I free to go?"***

Cop: *"No, you are not free to go. I'm detaining you."*

You: (Casually pulling out your micro-cassette recorder, pushing "record" and holding the microphone up:) ***"Oh, you're detaining me? What is your reasonable articulable suspicion?"***

Cop: (A bit rattled:) *"I don't have to tell you that."*

You: (Coolly:) *"Actually, you do. If you don't, it exhibits bad faith on your part--something both my lawyer and the court will frown on. As a _____ ("lawyer-in-fact," "paralegal," "legal scholar," "law student," etc.) I'm beginning to wonder if you indeed have any legal basis for stopping me. I'm asking you again to please articulate, for the legal record, your 'reasonable suspicion' for detaining me."*

Cop: (A bit flustered:) *"Your refusing to allow a search of your bag."*

You: (Cool but firm:) *"You need to catch up on the law, Officer. My re-fusal in no way gives you 'reasonable suspicion'--as* **U.S. v. Manuel** *ruled back in 1993. If you detain me based on that, then you're* personally liable *for an unlawful restraint. Now, unless you have some* actual *RAS, I'd like to go now."*

At this point, you've boxed him into a corner, and the cop must either: ❶ Let you go realizing that his bluff has failed and that pushing it will likely get him in trouble, or ❷ Articulate some true *"reasonable suspicion"* to support a lawful detention.

If he turns you loose, snort disgustingly and *leave.* While a smart parting line may seem irresistible, *don't.* You've already won, he *knows* it, and you must settle for that.   Later, you can raise a big stink, but then and there, just *leave.*

However, let's suppose that he *does* state some kind of valid RAS. If so, then he's got a lawful detention. Do not try to leave. Do not bluster or get upset. The situation (assuming you're behaving lawfully) is *still* in your favor 70/30. Stay calm, but increase your wariness. And *use* that little tape recorder!

The roust continues; what about concocted RAS?

How easy a thing it is to find a staff if a man be minded to beat a dog.
-- Thomas Becon, *Early Works: Preface* (1563)

Most RC's and many IC's *will* fudge on RAS if they feel that you're dirty and PC is likely, or if you've made a real nuisance of yourself. This is especially true if they are no friendly witnesses around. The old *"I detected the smell of marijuana."* is practically unbeatable, for example. (If this ever happened to me, I'd try to *immediately* dragoon some countering noses from the passersby. Put such a cop on the defensive, in front of witnesses, before he next "finds" something in your pockets. You must be very bold here. Cause a mild ruckus, proclaiming that you are being framed or set up.)

What if they try to move me during a detention?

Although you're *not* to be moved around during detainment, cops often do this (which elevates matters into an arrest).

Story in point: I know of somebody involved in a car accident and was later visited at work by the cops for routine questioning (mere contact). He was at his desk, carrying his pistol concealed in a gun fanny pack (which is lawful on one's own premises or at work). In what was probably a ruse, the cops asked him to follow them outside where they could "speak more freely." Once outside and in public, they (apparently knowing he was armed and having lured him into a trap) frisked him, confiscated his weapon and arrested him.

The only defense he has, in my opinion, is to assert that he was in actuality "taken in custody" (arrested) when moved outside (because he thought he had no right to refuse), even though cops had no RAS to detain, much less PC to arrest.

His pistol, however, is probably gone, regardless of a favorable ruling. (Even if erronously confiscated, guns are rarely returned any more.) If you conceal, at least carry something less stinging to lose, like a Russian Makarov for Ø140 or a Taurus .38 Special. It's silly to risk losing a tuned-up Colt Officer's Model, etc. Don't, however, sacrifice *too* much quality.

In retrospect, what he *should* have done was either refuse to leave his desk, or join them outside *after* he had discreetly left his pack behind. As I mentioned, it's always better to learn from the mistakes of *others*. **Don't *ever* allow a cop to trick**

or intimidate you into a worsened situation. Occupy the highest ground possible (preferably contact) and *stay* there while you effect an exit.

Some final thoughts on detentions

If you're detained, it means that you *blew* it--at least in some *small* way. Either you blew the contact when you *could* have simply walked away, or he detained you right off the bat (bypassing contact) because of your behavior. **You *blew* it.** Detention is the last step before arrest. Use wisdom and coolheadedness, and my Chapters 9-10 will be moot material.

A really shrewd cop will sometimes hold off on arresting (and therefore the required *Miranda* warning) even though he's *already* got PC to arrest. He'll briefly postpone arrest in order obtain more evidence from a talkative detainee (who usually doesn't know that he has the right *not* to answer questions). Once the suspect is actually arrested and *Mirandized*, the cop's chance of wheedling anything more are much reduced.

I mention this because *you* might sometime be detained when the cop already has PC to arrest. There's no way to reliably discern this, however. One solid clue is an overly confident, almost smug, attitude on his part. If the detaining cop seems unusually sure of himself and his questioning, he is likely to already have PC on you. I would then definitely answer his questions with, *"I have no knowledge of any crimes. I'd like to be on my way. **Am I free to go?**"* Run down the 20-30 minute clock of *"reasonableness"* with polite noncooperation and force him to either arrest or spring you.

A bit of *non-personalized* anger is often helpful here. The exact attitude to have is difficult to describe. Do not be snotty or sarcastic. Do not drop names or threaten a lawsuit. Do not stammer or avert your eyes. Do not clench your jaw, or cross your arms. **I'm trying to describe *anger without defiance.*** The cop is used to wimps and hotheads. By not being either, you will confuse him, and thereby create Doubt in his mind. By being gauntly cordial, and firm without fear, he will become unsure of himself, of the detention and of its consequences. If you do your part right, he *will* let you go. I've done it--I *know*.

- 8 -

SEARCH & SEIZURE

The right of the people to be secure in their persons, houses, papers, and effects, against unreasonable searches and seizures, shall not be violated, and no warrants shall issue, but upon probable cause, supported by oath or affirmation, and particularly describing the place to be searched, and the persons or things to be seized.
-- 4th Amendment to the Constitution

Most people believe that all searches by the police require a warrant. Ah, if only that were true. Although probable cause (PC) is thankfully still an overwhelming prerequisite, the courts have carved out many exceptions to the warrant requirement. For example, there are "searches" which are not technically searches, and there are even searches which are deemed *not* to require a warrant. Alas, the residue (searches requiring a warrant) is quite meager.

"SEARCHES" WHICH AREN'T REALLY SEARCHES

The 4th Amendment does not protect against searches of places and objects which anyone may see. A "search" within Constitutional contemplation means a police breach of private property. The following are not considered true searches:

Abandoned Property

When the owner forfeits his proprietary interest in something by leaving it in a public place, such is deemed to be discarded (as garbage thrown in a public trash can) or abandoned (as a junker car left on the road). The police may seize such abandoned property without a warrant or even PC.

Open Fields

You're gonna love this: cops may trespass onto your land and observe you from the undeveloped or unoccupied portion of your property which lies outside the *"curtilage of a dwelling."* What on earth does *"curtilage"* mean? The area around the home to which your home life extends.

What lies in/outside your own curtilage is solely within local judicial interpretation and your property's characteristics.

There are no hard and fast rules--only guidelines. ***Rosencranz v. U.S.,*** 356 F2d 310, 313 (1st Cir. 1966) and ***Wattenburg v. U.S.,*** 388 F2d 853, 857-8 (9th Cir. 1968) spelled out the:

Factors which tend to embrace a structure within the curtilage include:

1)   proximity or annexation to the house,

2)   *structures suggesting propinquity and absence of barriers (such as a driveway between the house and building),*
3)   *inclusion within the general enclosure surrounding the house,*
4)   *habitual use for family purposes, and*
5)   *indications that...owner sought to protect a privacy interest.*
-- E.X. Boozhie, *The Outlaw's Bible*; p. 127

An open area fenced in and posted with "No Trespassing" signs can be an "open field" outside the curtilage. While such entry may indeed be criminal trespass, it does not offend the 4th Amendment (which protects merely *privacy,* not possessory, interests). The police may trespass and snoop around your land just because it's not used as much as your porch or backyard. (Ah, it's nice to live in such a "free" country! America is merely the healthiest patient in the cancer ward, that's all.)

"Plain View"

The police may, without a warrant, seize any contraband or evidence of a crime that is in *"plain view"* **and to which he has lawful access.** If you invite a cop inside your home or business, you've given him the legal right to be there and anything seen in plain view can be seized. In public places and in your car, you have a *"lessened expectation of privacy"* and are much more vulnerable to plain view/hearing/smell seizures.

The only prerequisite is that the cop *must* have PC that the item to be seized is indeed contraband or evidence.

Aerial Surveillance

Well, let's say the cops want to look in your backyard, but can't because it lies within the curtilage. The solution is up, up and away. Cops can fly over your backyard and it's not a "search." If what they see gives them PC, they will easily obtain a search warrant.

What's more, minimum altitude requirements don't affect the constitutionality of the flyover any more than trespassing onto open fields does. Conceivably, a helicopter could hover 100 feet over your home, snapping photos with a telephoto lens of your interior activities. By the way, did I mention how nice it is to live in a "free" country?...

Controlled Deliveries

If the police have lawfully opened a container and identified its contents as contraband, they do not need a warrant to reopen it after a *"controlled delivery."* For example, if the postal workers "accidentally" discover (wink, wink) contraband mailed to you, the cops can reseal it, pose as your mailman for delivery, and arrest you.

If the cops *really* want somebody badly enough, they'll mail contraband to the mark and bust him. It appears that exactly this was done to federally licensed firearms dealer Al Woodbridge of Washington state. Incensed that Mr. Woodbridge was active in supporting the 2nd Amendment, machine gun parts were sent to him. When he signed for the unordered package (the contents of which were unknown to him), the BATF raided his shop. In an outrageous travesty of justice, he was convicted and is now serving time. **An indirect lesson here is: do *not* sign for unknown packages.** At least one fingerless victim of the Unabomber has learned this.

Private Searches

Only government officials are bound by the 4th Amendment. If a private Citizen discovers contraband within your property and tells the cops, they can follow up on the guy's intrusion with their own inspection. As long as the cops took no part in or encouraged the intrusion, they can use the information against you. *Beware* of whom you allow access to your property, such as guests, tenants, repairmen, salespeople, etc.

Impound and Post-arrest Inventories

Pursuant to departmental caretaking policy, a cop may conduct a warrantless inventory search of the passenger area, including glove box, of any lawfully impounded car. He may also open any closed containers for inventory purposes.

The same applies at the police station to the personal property (including closed containers) of an arrestee who is going to be booked and jailed. Heed Chapters 3 and 4!

SEARCHES WITHOUT A WARRANT

Now we arrive at true searches which *are* indeed within contemplation of the Constitution, but do *not* require a warrant. Many situations furnish the police with the PC necessary for a warrant, but not enough time to obtain a warrant beforehand. Such situations are called *"exigencies."* Cops may (with PC) search in a public place without a warrant to prevent evidence from disappearing. The exigency cannot be, however, of the cop's own making.

Emergencies
Another exigent exception to the warrant requirement is the protection of life and the rendering of aid. Such an exigency will allow the police to cross the 4th Amendment barrier. The most notable recent example of this was the L.A.P.D. homicide detectives climbing over the wall of O.J. Simpson's home, out of purported concern for his safety.

Conveniently overlooked at the show cause hearing were the detectives' blatantly contradictory actions once inside the walls. Instead of feverishly searching the home for injured persons and looking upstairs, they milled about, sniffing for clues. Clearly, Mark Fuhrman (who had responded to O.J.'s wifebeating years earlier) convinced the other detectives to rush over to O.J.'s. They had no real concern for O.J.'s safety, thus the "exigency" was a sham used to justify an illegal trespass and search. The prosecution managed to have the show-cause hearing judge (thoroughly out of her league and obviously overwhelmed) uphold the trespass, in the face of curiously lackluster defense objections. The jury seems to have seen through such (not to mention the perjury of Fuhrman) by acquitting after an astonishingly blink of four hours. This acquittal will have major shock waves in law and police procedure.

Hot Pursuit

This is also an exigency. For sake of public safety, cops may (with PC) search a building and arrest without warrant a suspect who is dangerous and/or feeing. Once a lawful arrest has begun, the cops are not rendered helpless merely because the suspect has fled to private property.

Search Incident to Lawful Arrest

As this is so closely related to an arrest, I discuss this search quite thoroughly in the Chapter 9, *The Arrest*. This search is ostensibly for inventory and protection purposes, but the cops love to find something extra after the arrest.

Automobile Searches

The *"automobile exception"* to the warrant requirement is well established. Since cars, planes, boats, etc. can be quickly moved while the police are obtaining a warrant, the courts have ruled that an exigency exists.

The cops may make a warrantless search of a car which was in motion, *or at least mobile*, when seized, and which they have PC to believe contains contraband or evidence of a crime-- even if the car has been taken into police custody (e.g.; the Lincoln search in *The French Connection*).

PC and the car's mobility must *both* exist *before* the seizure. If PC is discovered *after* the car is no longer mobile, or the car was *not* mobile *before* seizure, a warrant is necessary.

Such a search may extend to any part of the car, including closed containers, which may contain the object of the search. For example, a PC-based search for a stolen TV set cannot justify the opening of containers incapable of holding the TV set.

Cops will often cleverly wait until a suspect brings a "dirty" container out of his house into a public area or his car where it can be seized without a warrant. As long as the contraband remains *inside* a house or its curtilage, the cops will need a warrant to search and seize.

What about RV's and vans used as a home?

So long as they are *mobile* they will be treated as cars. However, RV's and travel trailers which are put up on blocks and connected to utility lines are most likely safe from the auto-mobile exception. (If you're concerned about this, take photos of its nonmobile status to prove your case later. Anything you can do to *decrease* its ready mobility, such as blocking it in or adding skirting, will strengthen your case.) "Mobile homes" are not readily mobile and require a warrant to enter.

Consent

I discuss consensual searches only in the interest of thoroughness. My readers are presumed bright enough to *never* consent to a search. There is the sticky possibility, however, of a household member consenting to a search of your home without your knowledge or express permission, so I will cover this.

The cops may conduct a search of property, even though they don't have a warrant or even PC, if they have obtained the prior consent of the one whose rights will be affected by the search, or of someone who has the right and the authority to act for the person whose rights will be affected by the search.

Consentor must have authority to permit the search.

The consentor must have, or *appear* to have, authority over the premises. Such authority usually exists if he has joint access or control over the place/thing to be searched.

Examples of where such authority is *lacking* are:
✘ A landlord over a tenant's premises.
✘ A hotelier over a guest's room during the rental period.
✘ An general employee over his employer's premises.
✘ An employer over his employee's exclusive premises.
✘ A young child over his home without his parents.

Examples of *unclear* authority are:
? Parents over room of adult offspring living at home.
? Person of doubtful authority (guest, baby-sitter, etc.).

The courts have *disagreed* about:
↔ Disputed amongst those with equal rights over the premises. Which prevails: one's consent or the other's refusal?

Consent must be positive. Silence is *not* consent.

Vague acquiescence is usually insufficient. *"I guess so"* is not generally considered consent. It must be clear and positive.

The search is limited to the extent of the permission.

The scope of the search is generally controlled by the what the cop and consentor said. If the cop says that he thinks that is a gun in the car and the driver consents to a search, the cop may not search places obviously incapable of concealing a gun.

Administrative Searches

Heavily regulated business (e.g.; junkyards, pawnshops, firearms dealers, mining operations, etc.) are probably subject to administrative inspections which require neither a warrant nor PC. Other licensed (privileged) professions are often subject to at least bookkeeping inspections. Anything seen by an official during a proper inspection is fair game.

This is an example of *"implied consent"*--a favorite tool used by government to get around the Bill of Rights. People are fooled into applying for licenses when such are *not* truly mandatory, and the government gets to claim implied consent because

of the actual voluntary nature of the license. By filing unre-
quired tax returns, you waive rights and oblige yourself to the
Internal Revenue Code. (My book *Good-Bye April 15th!* covered
this in great clarity and detail.) Beware of licenses--they're really voluntary privileges with many strings attached. Read the
fine print, for the devil is in the details.

Probation and Parole Searches

Probation and parole are voluntary agreements with the
government in lieu of prison time. Part of the agreement for
this release status is to be subjected to warrantless searches in
which RAS (much less PC) is rarely required.

SEARCHES NEEDING A WARRANT

The 9 pages of above exceptions aside, the only areas left
which require a search warrant is your home, non-licensed
business, and *maybe* locked containers in your car. Every place
else seems to fall into public plain view, a non-search, a *Terry*
frisk, an exigency, some implied consent, a *"search incident to
lawful arrest,"* or an *"inventory search."*

Though the police have historically whined that the warrant requirement hampers their work, such is clearly an ego-
centrically-based exaggeration. Cops generally see on the trees
and not the forest, and are understandably more concerned
about criminals getting away than any blanket infringement of
our rights. Most cops would prefer you to sacrifice your Liberty
to give them tools to catch criminals. I suggest that such
expediency is an extremely poor bargain.

Governments have caused (through their police and
military) *thousands* of times more property damage, injury and
death than mere criminals. Government has both a natural
propensity to control and a legal monopoly on force--historically
a disastrous combination. **Consequently, I'd *much* rather
suffer a small criminal class than a criminal *government*.**
Criminals I can more easily deal with...

So, the 4th Amendment provides a vital barrier to
sweeping arrests and searches by purposely interposing the
judiciary between the people and the executive. Just as a batter

cannot call his pitches, the police cannot decide for themselves whether or not to enter your house. The judge is an umpire.

Probable Cause

Probable cause to search is the existence of facts and circumstances that are enough to satisfy an officer of ordinary caution that a crime has been or is being committed, that the particular thing to be seized is reasonably connected to the crime, and that it can be found at a particular place.
    -- The Law Officer's Pocket Manual, BNA Books

All real searches, with or without warrant, require PC.

Constitutional Requirements

The search warrant is valid only if pursuant to a sworn affidavit setting forth the facts establishing PC to search particular premises for particular items. Sufficient detail is required, especially when describing papers to be seized. "All records" is unconstitutionally wide and vague.

Timeliness of information and execution is crucial. Stale information invalidates a search warrant, and a search warrant, once obtained, must be promptly executed.

Mistakes in the drafting or execution of search warrants will be overlooked as long as they are "reasonable." This doctrine was created to bypass the exclusionary rule, and is taken to terrifying new proportions in H.R. 666 (see Chapter 16).

Contraband not mentioned in the warrant but found in plain view may be seized. Remember, as long as the police have a lawful reason to be somewhere, plain view applies.

Oral Applications for Search Warrants

Telephonic applications for search warrants are now generally permissible if the situation makes a written affidavit impossible or impracticable. The feds may do so under Rule 41(c)(2) of the *Federal Rules of Criminal Procedure*.

The L.A.P.D., for example, obtained a telephonic warrant to search O.J. Simpson's home, though I can't see how a written affidavit was even impracticable much less impossible. I suspect abuse of these oral warrants, just as oral contracts are easily abused and misinterpreted.

- 9 -

THE ARREST

Ideally, you *should* have handled things better and *avoided* the arrest in the first place. I will stress this point often. After an arrest, lawful or unlawful, matters generally go downhill from there, as you're in the custody of adversaries. You've been "captured" and are now a "POW." Unfun...

The best course of action.

It's best to *avoid* an arrest, if such can be done without compromising your integrity and resoluteness. Don't take any crap, but it's generally foolish to expect granitelike repose 100% of the time. Remember, it's a "status/penis thing" with most cops. If you give them utterly *no* way to save at least a *bit* of face, they'll often push matters to the next level--arrest. *Sometimes* it's wise to back down a notch.

Unless you've got strong public pressure on your side, vigilant legal help (for a writ of *habeas corpus*, especially), and you can take care of yourself on the inside, an arrest will probably go rather poorly for you. It's not a guaranteed horror story, but you must have prepared for this possibility far in advance. I'm not trying to scare you into docility, but merely letting you know how it is.

If arrest is unavoidable.

An inescapable by-product of our modern tyranny is that some of us may indeed become martyrs, but don't go *begging* for that honor through wanton recklessness.

God made the angels to show Him splendor, as He made the animals for innocence and plants for their simplicity. But Man He made to serve Him wittily, in the tangle of his mind! If He suffers us to

*come to such a case that there is no escape, then we may stand to our tackle as best we can. And yes, Meg, then we can clamor like champions...if we have the spittle for it. But it's God's part, not our own, to bring ourselves to such a pass. **Our natural business lies in escaping.***
     -- from the 1966 Best Picture *A Man For All Seasons*

Involuntary martyrdom looms heavily enough without you "mooning" the State. **Besides, the "best" martyrs are *draftees,* not volunteers.** Don't be a hothead, not even for the worthy cause of Liberty. Be *"wise as serpents and harmless as doves"* as Matthew 10:16 advises. Being wise is not necessarily being wimpy. ***Cool* it and keep your wits about you.** Fight on *your* terms and *your* ground, not theirs.

This goes double for you leaders of American Liberty-- don't go salivating for some "hand to hand." This thing is a full-blown war, not a skirmish. We need wisdom, courage and stamina--not blind rage. We need you on the *outside.*

Legal basis for arrest / custody

Whenever a cop *"significantly restrains"* you, such *is* an arrest--even if he doesn't mean to actually arrest. Whether stemming from a warrant or exigent circumstances (or even a detention gone overboard), **any significant restraint (arrest) *must always* be supported by *"probable cause"* (PC).** Without PC, the cop may be liable for false arrest, and any evidence gathered is inadmissible in court (the "exclusionary rule"--now an endangered bulwark).

Defining *"probable cause"*

A landmark 1925 Supreme Court case (***Carroll v. U.S.,*** 267 US 132) ruled that PC is based on facts sufficient to warrant a reasonable *person* to believe that somebody has committed a crime. (While it takes a cop to say what is *"reasonable suspicion"* because a suspect's actions could be innocently interpreted by others--*anybody* can recognize what is PC.

The Colorado supreme court ruled in 1965 (***Gonzalez v. People,*** 177 Colo. 267) that *"one deals with probabilities."* A cop doesn't need the courtroom standard of *"proof beyond a reasonable doubt"* merely to arrest, he only needs reasonable probability.

What creates PC?

Generally, PC comes from evidence seen in *"plain view."* This doctrine also includes "plain hearing, smell, touch, etc." If the cop's five senses alert him to a crime, then he has PC. The important general standard is that the cop must personally *know* the factual situations involved. If he does not, then it is hearsay.

Can hearsay from an informant create PC?

While hearsay can *sometimes* establish PC, the standard is fairly strict. The cop must be able to explain:

❶ *why* the informant is a truthful, reliable person. (Special weight is given to "good citizens," victims of crimes, and cops. The courts do not normally believe: criminals, *quid pro quo* types, those with an "axe to grind," and the anonymous.)

❷ *how* he knows that the informant speaks from personal knowledge.

❸ *what* corroboration he has to confirm the informant's information.

When can a cop arrest with PC?

With PC, he doesn't need a warrant to arrest in public (on the road, at your public jobsite, on your front porch, etc.). When not in public (in your house or hotel room), he needs a warrant.

The cop's powers during a lawful arrest

He may use *"reasonable"* force to arrest--including up to deadly force, if necessary to prevent escape of a suspect whom the cop has PC to believe poses a significant threat to others.

He may conduct a *"search incident to arrest"* of your person and all places with your *"grabbable area"* plus an *"inventory search"* of your personal belongings and those inside your car.

He may even, during an *"exigency"* where a warrant is impractical, order a *"minor bodily intrusion"* if such procedure is reasonable in nature and reasonably conducted, and he has: PC to arrest, *and "clear indication"* (between RAS and PC) that evidence will be found. The most common example is the drawing of blood to determine alcohol levels. The cop is on *very* tenuous ground here and must tread carefully. While I abhor drunk driving as much as the next, I am quite shocked over such independent powers--powers sufficient to order the piercing of skin with a needle. *"Minor bodily intrusion"* indeed! Only today's courts could dream up such an Orwellian oxymoron.

Your rights during an arrest

Pretty minimal. You have the *Miranda* right to remain silent, or to *become* silent at any time. You have the right to an attorney (free of charge) and may speak to him before and during questioning. Generally, you may not be subjected to a *"major bodily intrusion"* such as a cavity or surgical search or forced vomiting without a warrant unless a real *emergency* exists (imminent danger to life or limb).

PRACTICAL TIPS DURING ARREST

If arrested I would take a firm defensive stand by saying something like the following, **and then *shut up:***

> I believe that I have a perfectly good defense, but I want to talk to my lawyer about it first. I understand that I have a right to remain silent, and a right to discuss my situation with a lawyer before saying anything to the authorities, and I intend to do just that. I intend to exercise my constitutional rights. Nothing personal, you understand.
>
> -- Univ. of Michigan Law Professor Yale Kamisar; *Supreme Court Review and Constitutional Law Symposium*, Washington, D.C., September 1982

I repeat: state the above and *shut up!* Your feet *had* their chance during contact, and *lost.* Your tongue had *its* chance during detention, and *lost.* **Now, *be quiet!***

What if it's clearly an unlawful arrest?

Though it seems only fair that one *should* be lawfully able to resist an unlawful arrest, such is not supported by the courts. In fact, resisting arrest (even an unlawful one) is an arrestable offense--so resisting a bad arrest will *give* it justification. **Therefore, do *nothing* to resist arrest.** "Resisting arrest" is the easiest thing for a bad cop to concoct, so beware. Cooperate physically or else he might include "resisting arrest" to cover himself. Do not complain at The Scene about the bum arrest, rather save your allegations for later, *after* all the charges have been made and it's too late for him to include "resisting arrest" *ex post facto*. This is only being shrewd.

The *"search incident to lawful arrest"*

The purpose for this search is to utterly ensure the cop's safety; to make certain that the arrestee has no hidden weapons. Also, the cop can seize any vulnerable evidence. There are three defining factors regarding this search:

❶ **Scope** (how *widely* he can search)--***Chimel v. California,*** 395 US 752 (1969)--limited this to the person of the arrestee and the area under his immediate control (the *"grabbable area"*).

❷ **Extent** (how *deeply* he can search)----***U.S. v. Robinson,*** 414 US 218 (1973)--allows a full field search of the above, including closed containers. Locked containers are generally off limits, as such require so much time to unlock/open that no immediate threat to the police can be reasonably presumed.

❸ **Timing** (*when* he can search)--must be *"contemporaneous"* with the lawful arrest, especially with regards to the surrounding area of the arrestee's car and home. Once in custody, these areas are generally off limits as the arrestee is presumably restrained from going for a weapon hidden in his glovebox, desk, etc. His *person,* however, may be searched even *after* arrest (e.g.; later at the police station), as he cannot be separated from his person (***People v. Boff,*** 766 P.2d 646 (Colo. 1988)).

Also, the cop may *not* conduct such a search unless he has *actually* arrested (in addition to merely detained) during those arrestable "cite-and-release" offenses (traffic tickets, jaywalking, having less than 1 oz. of pot, etc.) where he *may* arrest but chooses not to.

An implied lesson here is *not* to turn such a cite-and-release offense into an arrest. Unless your attitude is incredibly snotty or belligerent, you'll be cited and released. These discretionary arrestable offenses vary from state to state, so find out *prior* to being stopped.

Remember, these searches are incident to *lawful* arrest. If the arrest was *without* probable cause, or performed through either an invalid warrant or a valid warrant invalidly executed, or the arrest was not authorized for the offense--**the arrest**

and its incident search both fail. Evidence from such is called *"the fruit of the poisoned tree"* and is inadmissible.

The cop's powers in a *"search incident to arrest."*

As you might have gathered, they're quite extensive. He may even search unlocked closed containers if he can prove that the arrestee could have gotten to them during arrest (***New York v. Belton,*** 453 US 455 (1980), the landmark case on this point). *Generally,* locked containers are out of bounds, though expect some future inroads to be made here. The so-called *"grabbable area"* can be *very* widely construed, usually including your car's passenger compartment, though *not* the trunk unless you are standing next to it during arrest and it's open-able *without* a key (***Robbins v. California,*** 453 US 420 (1981)). Within these parameters, *anything* found is fair game.

Your rights during a *"search incident to arrest."*

Pretty thin. Only major bodily intrusions (cavity and surgical searches) and locked containers require actual warrants. The police are *not* supposed to move you about in order to increase the scope of their search (***U.S. v. Griffin,*** 537 F.2d 900 (7th Cir. 1976)).

Practical tips during a *"search incident to arrest"*

The best advice, obviously, is to avoid being arrested in the first place. Barring that, I hope you'd taken my preparatory steps so that such a search turns up nothing useful to the police, like locking all your stuff in the trunk.

Barring *that*, the only general advice I can give is not to widen your *"grabbable area"* by voluntarily changing locations (e.g.; going from sidewalk to your car, from outside your home to inside, or from inside one room of your home to another room.).

If an arrest seems likely, try to smoothly eliminate your property (car, home, business, etc.) from your *"grabbable area"* during the contact or detention stage--before actually being arrested. This area is defined *during* the actual arrest, not before, so you'll probably have a brief window of opportunity if the cop is not suspicious.

I did this very thing when stopped for speeding and I knew that I had an outstanding warrant for an unresolved ticket.

While the cop radioed me in, I discreetly secured my pistol and papers in a locked case. After cuffing me, he went through my car thoroughly but couldn't breach the locked case, to his disappointment. After this, I learned to take earlier and more detailed preparations and *not* let old tickets go unresolved.

The *"inventory search"*

This applies only to property on the arrestee's person, and in his impounded car (though generally not including locked containers). The ostensible purpose is to protect your valuables, as well as cover the police in case of theft claims. But let's face it: the real, unstated co-purpose is to *snoop.*

The vehicle inventory search is legally complex and potentially the most detrimental to you, and that's why you *should* have pulled over in a private parking lot. The inventory search has, predictably, been quite abused by cops who use it for a pretext to search when they have no PC to search or can't search as thoroughly during a mere *"search incident to lawful arrest."*

Consequently, the courts generally require that less intrusive means than impoundment to secure the car be used rather. If it's legally parked, or may be legally parked close by, it can be locked up and left there. Or, it may be released to a sober passenger with a valid drivers license. Or, you might be able to call a friend and have it picked up quickly, though this will take some powerful persuasion on the cop (and maybe on your friend, too). I've gone through the impound thing twice, and it's a real hassle. Avoid it if you can.

If your car is either empty or packed to the roof, the cops may not even bother with an inventory search.

SEARCH OF CAR

LEGAL THEORY	REQUIREMENTS	Searchable Area
Consent	valid consent from person with *"joint access"* to car	anywhere consentor allows
Plain View	lawful presence; PC to believe evidence is crime-related; inadvertence	is not a search; may enter car to seize
Terry *frisk* (*Search Incid. to Detention*)	specific, explainable fear for safety *and* reason to believe weapon is in a particular reachable area of car	any area(s) where detainee could reach to get weapon
Probable Cause	PC to believe evidence is in car; warrant or exigency	areas authorized by warrant or exigency, where evidence could be located
Auto Exception	PC *and* mobility	anywhere evidence could be located
Search Incident to Lawful Arrest	valid custodial arrest	passenger area including unlocked, closed containers
Inventory Search	lawful custody	anywhere except sealed containers

SEIZURE OF CAR OCCUPANT

	EVIDENCE REQUIRED	COP'S POWER	SUSPECT'S RIGHTS
CONTACT	none	none (car must already be parked)	free to drive/walk away or ignore cop
DETENTION	traffic offense; or RAS of a crime	move driver to curb; ask questions; frisk with reasonable, explainable fear	free *not* to answer questions or give ID; free to go if no PC; can't be *"significantly restrained"* unless exigency
ARREST	PC that he committed crime	search incid. to arrest; handcuff; inventory of car; book	remain silent; make phone call; see an atty.; *habeas corpus*

- 10 -

AFTER THE ARREST: THE INTERROGATION, ETC.

After the arrest, while being held

Do what they say. Be polite, not snotty. Such often lowers their guard, and may provide you some unexpected advantage. Besides, politeness can go far as it's so uncommon in jail. Who knows?--a sympathetic soul might even do something kind for you. **A poor attitude *cannot help* in the slightest.** You're already in *custody* (in the control of others) so don't make it worse. Once free, *then* you can get "uppity."

Say *nothing*. They're already so convinced of your guilt that they *arrested* you, remember? **Nothing you can say will change that. There is simply *no* talking your way out of it, so don't even *try*.** You might inadvertently give them something helpful. Also, you don't want to alert them to your legal strategies or any deficiencies in their case, however tempting it may seem to gain the upper hand, even if for a moment. Save this properly for later, as a *surprise*.

Sign *nothing*. Signatures always imply *agreements*. If the law truly requires something of you without your consent, then no signature is needed. Beyond an accurate and detailed inventory checklist of your belongings, sign *nothing*. **This goes *triple* for any form of probation or deferred adjudication.** The State offers these deals only when their case is weak. Stick it out for a *total* victory, if you can.

Beware of "favors." Behind bars it's a *quid pro quo* (this for that) world, and by accepting a "favor" you'll be obligate yourself to returning one, usually at steep "interest."

Making post-arrest phone calls

Jail phones are usually monitored, so beware. Unless you call your lawyer, consider setting up a relay instead of directly calling your home (which should be *private* to all but close friends and family). What I mean by a relay, is a friend who is nearly always at home who can/will take your "I've been arrested" call and relay such to somebody who goes from there. The purpose of the relay is to keep your home, business, etc. unknown to the authorities.

THE INTERROGATION

Nancy Lord and I are both of the firm opinion that **arrestees should: *never* answer questions and *always* demand an attorney.** Though the police are then *required* to cease their questioning, this *doesn't* always happen--so you'll need to know how to resist a continued interrogation.

To avoid "reinventing the wheel" I'll paraphrase Jack Luger's *Ask Me No Questions--I'll Tell You No Lies* (ISBN 1-55950-072-7 from Loompanics) which has good, basic info.

Techniques of applying pressure

The first and most important task of the interrogator is to get you to *talk*. Without you, he has only a monologue. Remember, he *needs* you to talk. The State's case is incomplete and they want you to charitably fill it in. Don't worry if the police want to question you. **Be extremely nervous if they *don't*.**

Rapport
This is lull you into lowering your guard. He will be friendly, polite, and seemingly believing. Don't buy it! If he was your friend, he'd let you go home without a grilling.

Conditioning
This stage is to get you to answer questions in general. He'll begin with asking for routine, non-damaging information such as your name, address, and phone number. This is a seductive technique since there's no apparent harm in telling him what you think he already knows. Beware, he truly may *not* know much of the basic information. **Think *before* opening your mouth--and then, think *again*.** If you balk, he'll say it's only to verify his information. Call his bluff and ask to see his file on you and you'll personally correct any erroneous data.

He's also trying to establish a "baseline" of behavior as he notes your reactions. He'll carefully watch your eyes, expression, posture and body language. Later, when the critical questions come, he'll be alert for behavior changes to denote stress.

Repetition and Fatigue
He will try to wear you down by hammering the same questions again and again to force you: first to talk, and then to make mistakes and inconsistencies. Keep your polite silence!

Verbal Tricks
There are a few pat lines he'll try on you:

"I just need you to answer a few routine questions."
You'll hear this during the "conditioning" phase. "Routine" questions are *never* innocuous or unimportant.

"I'm only trying to help you."
This is *prima facie* B.S. Ask to be set free--*that's* "helpful!"

"I want to give you a chance to tell your side of the story."
Demand *their* version of the "story" without telling yours.

"What are you trying to hide?" (Presumes guilt.)
Reply, *"What are you trying to make me say?"*

"Innocent people don't mind answering questions."
Flatly reply that it's *because* you're innocent that you're not going to stick your head in somebody else's noose.

"You'll feel better if you talk to me." (Presumes guilt.)
Reply that your conscience is perfectly clear.

"You lied before. Why should I believe you now?"
Simply deny that you've lied.

Intimidation
He could dispense with any rapport altogether and begin as a "hardass." Scowling, long periods of hopefully uncomfortable silence, staring you down, and good-cop-bad-cop ploys are to be expected. It's all melodrama, so don't let it get to you.

Squeezing For More
A basic technique is to say "and" whenever you stop speaking, which suggests that you have more to tell. Say, *"That's it. I've nothing else to say without my attorney."*

Expect predicated questions such as, *"When did you first start breaking the law?"* or something of that nature. Firmly deny the unstated assumption and clam up.

Single word questioning is used to goad elaboration. If you say that you were with a friend last night, he'll say, *"Friend?"* and simply stare at you. Say, *"Yes, friend."*

Bluff and Deceptive Tactics

Since the rack is out (generally), deception is in. At least half of any interrogation is pure bluff. Expect these lines:

"Your partner's already told us everything." or,
"We already know everything, so you just confess."
Reply, *"Well, if so, then you don't need my story, do you?"*

"They just identified you."
This can be a lie or a totally faked demonstration. Call their bluff, *"Oh, darn! See you in court then."*

"This is your last chance for a deal."
Don't fall for this false sense of urgency. Such is B.S. unless the prosecutor signs a statement with your attorney there.

The Covert Interrogation

This takes place outside formal interrogations in settings which one would expect are safe.

Infiltrators and False Friends

They will try to worm into your life and get you to say something damaging. Suspect any new people, especially those who seem *too* agreeable, sympathetic and like-minded.

Undercover Cellmate

A cop poses as a criminal suspect and is placed in your cell. No *Miranda* warning is necessary during this ruse.

COPING WITH THE SQUEEZE

With enough time and pressure, *anybody* will crack. Silence is the best route, for once you start answering questions the rest is easy for him. Many POW's know this personally.

How Well Can You Resist?

How *vulnerable* are you to intimidation? You must examine your personality and honestly appraise yourself. If you are easy to manipulate, suggestible and willing to talk--you of all people should *absolutely* demand a lawyer and shut up.

Can you stand silence when with another person, or do you feel a need to break the silence and say something?

Do you listen carefully when another speaks to you, or do you just wait for him to finish so that you can talk?

Do you crave attention, or prefer to be ignored?

Do you contact your friends as a rule, or do they call you? Do you need people more than they need you?

Are you suggestible? If someone says, *"Look at that,"* do you immediately turn your head?

Do you snap out your answers to questions?

Do you often need to explain and justify yourself?

Are you the "nervous" type, and do you show it by gestures and movements of the hands and feet?

How good is your resistance to discomfort?

Do you have a criminal record? This is vital in determining how investigators treat you.

What is your ethnicity? Certain races typically commit certain crimes, and he will look for stereotypical suspects.

What is your socioeconomic level? The more poor you are, the more you are assumed to be ignorant of your rights.

Avoiding Emotional Isolation

If subjected to a post-arrest interrogation, you will be separated from your friends and family. You won't have a lawyer unless you demand one. You'll be on the cops' turf, not your own. Realize this in advance and remember: the interrogation is only temporary. Stay silent and keep your wits about you.

Presenting A Credible Front

Most important is your overall image of respectability. A shady guy could actually tell the truth and be disbelieved, while a con-man exuding sincerity could be lying. Even though you should never answer questions, you should cultivate a *believable* air. This will likely reduce the length and ardor of the interrogation, and help cool their presumption of your guilt.

Eye Contact
Maintain eye contact. Don't let your eyes move differently when really grilled.

Speech
Regulate your tone and cadence. Avoid "ums" and "ahs."

Assertiveness
Be assertive without offensiveness. Such requires poise. Be polite, but don't take any crap or "bulldozing."

Body Language
Practice relaxing. Don't fidget, or tap your foot. Relax.

Preparation
If you're due for an interrogation, try to pre-enact the stress beforehand. If you keep a polite silence, you can't be tricked into hesitating, equivocating or evading.

Tactical Resistance
Techniques are to deny-deny, shake your head whenever the interrogator begins to speak, and appear confused.

Exploiting Interrogator's Mistakes
Always have him give away more information than he gets. Analyze his questions to glean what he knows.

Don'ts

Don't volunteer information.
Supplying additional information leads only to additional questions. Make him ask you directly about something.

Dont display a *sullen* silence.
Keep quiet, but be *cordial* (though not friendly).

Don't adopt an unusually calm, emotionless manner.
This is unnatural and offensive to most people. Show reasonable, proper emotion for the situation.

Don't be flip or a smartass during the interrogation.

This conveys the attitude that you don't take him or his questions seriously, and makes it a Personal Thing.

Don't shoot your mouth off.

Remember, silence is golden, even if others say it's yellow.

SOME FINAL TIPS

If you are moved about and questioned by different cops, you should *restate* your choice of silence and demand for an attorney to *everybody who questions you.* Nobody in the entire building should be able to claim they "didn't know" of your invoking the Fifth Amendment. Sound like a worn record, *"I didn't do anything wrong, and I have nothing to say without my attorney present."*

If you wisely invoke your right to silence with demand for an attorney and are *still* subjected to an unlawful inter-rogation, this should be of *great* concern to you. Such post-silence interrogations are *very* risky for the police, and you should strongly wonder *why* they are chancing a fat lawsuit (which you are almost guaranteed to win).

Be *extremely* on guard here. If they belatedly realize their error, they might try to set you up while inside to pressure you into not going after them. Beware of something planted on you or in your cell.

I would immediately file a writ of *habeas corpus* to get before a judge and describe your unlawful treatment. If you are unconstitutionally prohibited from doing so, have somebody on the outside file on your behalf. **You *must* bring swift and intense legal pressure to bear *ASAP*. Go on the *offensive*--wars are *never* won through purely defensive postures.** Try to get media attention if you're a "political" prisoner, or if the arrest is a pretextual sham. When the DA "feels the heat" he will probably "see the light." Good luck!

- 11 -

AT THE AIRPORT

In my experience, the airport is most vulnerable place one normally occasions. It is the epitome of controlled environments, in which you've voluntarily entered and thus given *'implied consent."* Nobody there has in mind your privacy or rights. You are under pressure to make your flight under the gauntlet of surveillance.

For a full portent of times to come, experience the new Denver International Airport (DIA). It reminds one of the airport in the futuristic movie *The Running Man.* The place literally sags with cameras and questions, cattle chutes and the cold efficiency of Buchenwald. DIA is so abhorred that many Denverites choose to drive the 60 miles and fly from Colo. Springs.

I'd personally rather risk the decennial terrorist or two than be subjected to the dystopian indignity of more DIA's. The golden age of air travel is *over.* Commercial flight is now an Orwellian neo-fascist ordeal, as is simply motoring down the "free"way. First, they've got to make it a tribulation to travel, even domestically. Next, they'll try to bring regulatory grief to your porch. The goal? **To make us miserable enough-- hopeless enough--to *obey.***

This philosophical venting accomplished, let's consider airports and the police, shall we? The primary risk you take at airports is being contacted and detained by the drug cops. Not because you are carrying drugs, but because you might unknowingly fit the "profile" of a courier. Even though this allegedly highly accurate "profile" results in only a 60% success rate (barely more than a coin toss), the courts still allow "profiles" to justify RAS and thus a detention.

THE DRUG COURIER "PROFILE"

I'm going to cover the "profile" inversely: instead of describing what it is, I'll tell you what behavior to avoid. Much of the following comes from *The Outlaw's Bible* by E.X. Boozhie, who compiled the first, and probably best, list. I include this information, not to assist drug traffickers, but to help the rest of you make your flights without undue hassle.

Avoid being attired:
✈ differently from other passengers.
✈ inappropriately for the weather.
✈ in the same clothes as when you left.
✈ shabbily, or so as to reveal strange bulges.

Avoid travelling alone, or:
✈ without luggage, especially on a long trip.
✈ with empty, or untagged tagged luggage.
✈ with padlocks on your luggage.
✈ with a shoulder bag.
✈ with luggage inappropriate for your destination.

Avoid flying:
✈ from a "drug source city."
✈ at off-peak hours.
✈ on a round-trip ticket with a short layover.
✈ on a ticket with a peculiar itinerary.

Avoid purchasing your ticket:
✈ at the ticket desk.
✈ on the same day as your flight.
✈ with cash (particularly small bills).
✈ changing flights enroute.

Don't act suspiciously, like:
✈ scanning, or cloak-and-dagger stuff.
✈ cautious, hesitant, nervous, or furtive behavior.
✈ inordinate haste, or killing time inappropriately.
✈ going directly to the telephone.
✈ avoiding your travelling companions.

An ordinary traveler (whom you presumably want to be taken for) generally has one of two objectives on his mind when he enters the airport: (1) to get his ticket and get to the proper boarding gate, or (2) to meet his greeting party and pick up his luggage. ...He's likely to be cheerful, enthused about his trip, and generally cordial toward airline personnel and security police alike; after all, he has no reason to fear the police.
     -- E.X. Boozhie; *The Outlaw's Bible*, p. 284

When returning home from abroad:

Avoid making short trips abroad, or returning directly from a "drug source country."

With regard to your airline ticket:
+ Avoid purchasing it with cash.
+ Know when/where/how it was purchased.

Avoid travelling:
+ alone, particularly if you're a Latin woman.
+ with only a small piece of luggage.

Don't exhibit:
+ Extreme passivity/indignation, or nervousness.
+ Talkativeness or extreme helpfulness with Customs.

Appear to be dependent on checks and credit cards.
+ Carry a checkbook, traveler's checks and credit cards.
+ Avoid carrying large sums of cash.

Have a *plausible* story if asked by U.S. Customs.
+ Have a sight-seeing itinerary if claiming tourism.
+ If on business, be able to prove it with details.

Miscellaneous tips of my own:
A combination of several of these "profile" characteristics will probably cause a DEA agent to accost you to "ask a few questions." Politely ask to see his credentials. After writing down his name and ID#, return it, politely refuse his "invitation" and walk away. He must either detain or arrest to prevent

you from leaving. He will want to see your ID and ticket. During contact and detention, you may (and should) *refuse*.

Don't look like this!

If your bag is detained and you don't want to be around when they sniff it, firmly state your possessory right to it, explain that you'll return with your attorney to retrieve it, and leave the airport. Cash and other sensitive items you should keep on your person, anyway.

If carrying lots of cash, remove the platinum-lettered strips embedded in the >1990 bills--they set off detectors.

To foil or delay searches is to put your cash and papers in a Priority Mail Tyvek envelope affixed with postage and safe address. Only postal inspectors with PC can open it. Really sensitive stuff should be mailed ahead.

Guns may be legally transported in your check-through luggage if they're unloaded, in a locked hard case, and declared to the ticket agent. You'll sign an orange tag which reads, *"I declare, as required by the Code of Federal Regulation 108.11, that the firearm(s) being checked as baggage is (are) unloaded."* I've never found it to be a big deal. Others do, and sprinkle about their field-stripped pistol without declaring it. Checked bags are rarely X-rayed, so the odds of this working are nearly 100%.

Before landing from overseas, fill out *two* U.S. Customs cards identically. On the ground, if you are accosted by a roving Customs agent who views you suspiciously, he will ask for your card, and scribble some cryptic notation--alerting the desk agent to thoroughly search your stuff and really grill you. Pocket that card and present the *other* one, which hasn't any such notations. (A tip from personal experience! BTP)

- 12 -

AT THE CHECKPOINT

These include random sobriety checkpoints, license checks, Border Patrol checkpoints fixed miles inside the U.S.A., agricultural checkpoints, etc. If you wander in one of these ongoing fishing expeditions, the courts generally "reason" that you *chose* to as alternative routes were available.

The "Checkpointeers" are permitted to ask you their basic questions, and once answered they *must* allow you to pass-- unless they have RAS to detain or PC to search or arrest.

Not all, however, will let you go so easily. INS agents are the worst offenders. I once had to pass through one of their "temporary" Border Patrol checkpoints located far inland. While they are quite fixed and elaborate, the Supreme Court ruled in *U.S. v. Martinez-Fuerte*, 428 US 543 (1976) that they cannot be operated 365 days--thus the "temporary." Anyway, after ascertaining that I was an American, "GreenMan" asked where I was headed. *"North,"* I boredly answered.

INS:	*"Well, I know that, but what's your destination?"*
Me:	(Indignant:) *"That's a rather personal question!"*
INS:	(Now hostile:) *"What's in your trunk?"*
Me:	(Firmly:) *"Lawful personal property."*
INS:	*"Open it!"*
Me:	(Flatly:) *"No."*
INS:	(Leaning into my face, menacingly:) *"No?"*
Me:	(Even more flatly, almost yawning:) *"That's correct, no."*

By that time his partner had joined him and they barraged me with *"What's in your trunk? Whose car is this? Where did you come from?"* and questions of similar ilk. I cut them short with:

Me: (Resolutely:)   *"Gentlemen, I am a law-abiding Citizen going about my lawful business. I am carrying no contraband. I've committed no crime. **Unless you can state probable cause to the contrary for the benefit of my tape-recorder here, I shall be on my way.**"*

The microcassette recorder to IC's is like a cross to Dracula. They totally deflated and backpedaled their way out:

INS: (Effusively:)   *"Oh, hey, we weren't trying to hassle you! Haven't you ever been through here before?"*   (Translation: *"Why don't you whimper at our every command?"*)
Me: (Sternly:)   *"Yes, I've passed through here before, and I cannot recall ever being treated with such disrespect!"*

All they wanted right then was for me to drive away, which I did amongst their profuse *"Bon voyages."* **The lesson: know your rights and *assert* them.** Americans need to stop rolling over and peeing on their bellies as cowering puppies! **Enough of this wimpery!** Men--start acting like men! Ladies--*shame* these thugs into treating you as ladies.

Avoid driving near Can/Mex borders:
    ✗ in an enclosed truck, van, or station wagon.
    ✗ with numerous passengers.
    ✗ on infrequently travelled roads.

When crossing borders, avoid driving:
    ✗ alone, especially if you're an elderly man.
    ✗ a rented car, or with out-of-state license plates.
    ✗ an empty car.

Beware the federal areas
Military bases, National forests and parks, Indian reservations and federal offices are all bits of federal territory wherein your Constitutional rights are barely recognized. Try to avoid these areas if you can. If you can't, then prepare yourself and your property *very* thoroughly. The federal zone is hostile territory.

- 13 -

RED LIGHTS ARE FLASHING

Make no furtive or sudden moves. Stay *calm*.

Cops love to closely follow a "hinky" driver in hopes of rattling him. Stay cool and collected. Don't start rearranging your car's entire interior--that should have been done earlier.

Quickly and smoothly secure any unlawfully carried weapons, lock up your personal effects in the briefcase, and perform the next bit, if you can.

If you're *about* to be pulled over, *beat him to it*.

The less you drive in his presence, the fewer "traffic infractions" he can allege and the fewer pretexts he can concoct to detain you. In fact, I make a rule of not allowing the police behind me, not even for a few blocks. I keep them in front of me always.

Act like you don't see him, pull over at some business, get out, lock up your car and walk away. Act surprised when he pulls up behind you. By separating yourself from your car *before* he lit up his lights you've made it more difficult for him to involve your car and contents in his snooping.

When pulled over, do so in a private parking lot.

The reason for this is that if you *are* arrested, your car can more than likely remain, rather than be impounded off the street and subject to an *"inventory search"* For-Your-Protection (wink, wink). If you've no cell phone, try to pull over near a pay phone. That way, if The Scene turns dicey and your arrest is likely, you can call a friend to come fetch your car and let him know where you will be taken. If possible, ask the store manager for permission to leave your car on his lot until your friend arrives shortly. (Allay his fears with the explanation that it's merely an unpaid ticket causing all the hassle.)

Have any cover story already prepared.

The basic thing is to keep it simple, benign, and in *agreement*. You're on your way to the mall to buy some sheets, whatever. My own pat story is coming from K-Mart where I was looking for, with no success, some metric allen bolts. (There's even a missing such bolt under my hood, if need be.) This is perfectly benign *and K-Mart never has them*.

"Where am I going? Well, to some hardware store; any suggestions, Officer?") Do you see the beauty in that? **I'm on a routine, boring mission which explains where I've been and where I'm going.** Make up your own, like searching for an exotic brand of hot sauce (which nobody carries). It's defensible, different enough to sound true, yet offers *nothing*.

You want to sew up The Scene quickly and firmly, leaving him with no secondary inquiries to make. Remember the highway patrolman who pulled up while I was unsticking a choke? I initiated the confrontation, explained in 8 seconds--leaving the issue closed--and walked back. Nothing about my car or demeanor was suspicious, so he had nowhere to go but away.

You are *not* going to: the airport, the gun range, a friend's house, etc. All these destinations invite further questions: *"Really, where are you flying to?"* or *"Oh, so you have guns in this car?"* or *"Which friend?"* Once you start stammering to these follow-up queries, you're in for a *real* grilling. Have a simple story which contains its own beginning and ending. Leave him no place to go. And make sure that your passenger can play along.

Start the "clock" ticking.

Time is not on his side, and he's banking on you not knowing this. If your watch has a stopwatch feature, click off when his lights begin flashing. He's got an easy 20 minutes. After 20 minutes it becomes increasingly more difficult to justify detaining you (especially when you don't operate as your own enemy). If the detention looks flimsy in court, a cop will usually understate the length of detention. Forty minutes becomes 25, and 15 minutes was "only 5 to 7." Have credible evidence to counter this eventuality.

While I've rarely been held for as long as even 20 minutes, it's happened. If he seems to be stretching it out regardless of his time window, remind him that the "sand is running out" and point to your stopwatch. *"Officer, we both know that you can't detain me forever. Shall we be on our ways now?"*

Get out coolly and lock your car door behind you.

Generally, the cop will order you *out* of the car anyway, as it's safer for him. His power to do so was held in **Pennsylvania v. Mimms,** 434 US 106 (1977) and many other cases.

Get out naturally without waiting or asking. By doing so, you've separated your person from the interior of your car (which otherwise is considered within your *"grabbable area"*). Since the courts have held that the cop's safety is paramount to your 4th Amd. right, the cop can *Terry* frisk your person and any area functionally within your *"grabbable area"* (e.g.; an unlocked car, nearby surroundings, etc.) for weapons.   By locking your door, you've made the entire car as inviolate as the trunk, which cannot be searched without PC.

It is *not* guaranteed that you will always be allowed to exit. In fact, a particular court case (***People v. Harrison,*** 443 N.E.2d 447 (1982)) ruled that the cop *may* legally order you back *into* your car. Such can be a clever move on his part since it automatically increases your *"grabbable area"* and thus the area of a *Terry* frisk or *"search incident to arrest."* You want to be *out* of the car for the same reason a snooping cop wants you *in.* Quickly getting out will make many cops suspicious. **Get out *coolly*, and return *without a fuss* if he tells you to.**

I had an interesting opportunity to test this last year. **Boston's real-life incident #1:** A rather shrewd highway patrolman in an unmarked car managed to pace me at 75+ and thus not activate my radar detector.   I quickly secured my belongings as described, pulled over, got out, locked my door behind me, and walked back. (The interior of my car was spotlessly clean and totally empty. My trunk, however, was packed with personal belongings.) To my surprise, he asked me to wait in my car.   (I couldn't remember this *ever* having happened. I always get out and leisurely walk back.) Anyway, The Scene went like this:

Me: *"I'd rather wait outside. My AC doesn't work and I'm hot."*
Cop: *"Well, I still need you to wait inside your car."*
Me: *"Look, I've been on the road all day, I'm hot and I'm getting cramped up in there. I'd rather wait outside and stretch my legs."*
Cop: *"Yes, but please just wait in your car. This won't take long."*
Me: *"But why can't I simply walk around and stretch my legs?"*
Cop: (Annoyed:) *"Sir, it's for safety's sake. Please wait inside."*

Me: (Pushing the issue, out of curiosity:) *"Well, I'm not concerned with my safety, and if you're concerned about yours, you can give me a* Terry *frisk--I'm not armed or anything."*
Cop: (Clearly surprised at my firmness and knowledge of *Terry:*) *"Sir, I'm not going to tell you again! Get back in your car!"*
Me: (Really pushing it now:) *"Is this a request or legal demand?"*
Cop: (Now annoyed and suspicious:) *"It's a legal demand. What is this--is there something in your car you don't want me to see?"*
Me: (Walking back to the car:) *"No, I'm just tired of being cooped in here, that's all. Also, I wasn't sure if you were asking me or telling me."*
Cop: (On a hunch:) *"You wouldn't have a gun in there, would you?"*
Me: (Coolly:) *"As I said, officer, I'm not armed. I just preferred to be outside and walk around in the fresh air."*

Obviously, I brought on his suspicion by pressing the issue of staying outside. When he saw that I had to unlock the door to get in, he was *really* on alert. Remember, this was an *intentional* test case, with full expectation of his likely reaction. I gave him my paperwork through the driver's window, he radioed a check on me, and (as I later realized) requested backup. After about 7 minutes he returned, and said I could step out of my car. I got out, again locked the door behind me and walked back. To my initial surprise, he explained that he was going to merely give me a warning on the speeding. As I quickly understood, this was not out of generosity, but to soften me up for the next stage:

Cop: (Handing me the warning ticket:) *"Here you are. Please watch your speed. Say, would you mind if I looked under your seat?"*
Me: (Unemotionally:) *"What would you be looking for?"*
Cop: *"I believe you have a pistol under your seat."*
Me: (Not flustered, but a touch indignant:) *"As I've already said, officer, I'm not armed. I have nothing to do with drugs; I have no contraband in the car. There's nothing there to concern you."*
Cop: (Somewhat taken aback:) *"So you're refusing consent?"*
Me: (Pleasant, though firm:) *"That's right. I never waive my rights , and in fact, I'm a bit insulted by all this."*
Cop: (Cajolingly:) *"Oh, you wouldn't be waiving your rights! You'd just be cooperating! Who told you it's waiving your rights?"*
Me: *"My attorneys. I travel on business and they counseled me on this a long time ago, because I was curious. There's nothing to be gained by me waiving my rights, even if I have done something wrong--which I haven't."*

Cop: (Realizing consent was impossible, and "getting tough":)   *"You know that I can call for a drug-sniffing dog, don't you?"*
Me: (Calling his bluff:)   *"Oh? How will a drug-sniffing dog alert to a gun, which is just a piece of steel?"*

With that he marched back to his radio to call for a dog. Just then a colleague of his showed up, and I then realized that he had been on his way minutes earlier. The 2nd cop was very cool and we made pleasant conversation. *Many* times have I indirectly softened up a ticked off cop by simply being polite with his colleague. If the first cop is an IC or RC, try to bring out "Good Cop" in his partner. Once, a *real* RC (who was planning to set me up) was so incensed by my casual attitude that his partner actually took him aside and talked some sense into him. Happily, a very dicey stop was defused.)

After 5 minutes, the 1st cop returned and said that I was free to go as the dog was too far away (to arrive within a *"reasonable"* time of 20-30 min.).

A word of advice here: when being released after a heavy Scene, don't become overtly happy and relieved--that implies guilt. **Soften, *but don't cancel*, your aura of indignation. Make *them* glad to be rid of *you*, not vice versa.** Don't blow your release by getting all giddy.

Anyway, I extended my hand, shook his, thanked him for the warning on the speeding ticket and said:

Me: *"Look, you haven't missed anything here. I'm not up to anything. I just believe in standing up for my rights. Nothing personal, O.K.?"*
Cop: (Holding back a grin:)   *"Yeah, well, let me explain the laws around here regarding a pistol in your car. You can carry in your car as long as it's in a holster and left either under your seat or in the glovebox."*
Me: (If so, then what was this whole Scene about?, I wondered to myself.)   *"Well, Officer, I can assure you that if I were to travel with a pistol in my car, it would be secured exactly in the manner you just described."*

He and his partner couldn't help but chuckle at that. I bid them good day and drove off. In retrospect, it couldn't have ended better: I avoided a search *and* got off with a warning.

The lesson here is to learn *beforehand* if the cop can order you back to your car. (I didn't know and purposely pushed it to find out.) If they can, get out anyway, and *if* they order you back, comply without a fuss. Your car interior *should* be able to withstand a frisk or search, anyway--if necessary.

If he seems to want to go through the interior, try to lock and close the door behind you as you get out. If it's *serious* and he's hovering right by your door ready to pounce inside, try to quickly get out of the *passenger* door. This will make him *freak*, and is a *last* resort when your car interior isn't secured.

If, in your city/state, carrying a gun in your car is lawful, then consider this sudden idea: Secure your pistol as described in Chapter 4, get out and lock the door behind you. If he orders you back inside, reply, *"Oh, I thought you'd feel safer with me outside and my pistol remaining inside the car."* For him to *then* order you inside would contradict any purported concern for his own safety. If he demands to check out the pistol, reply that carrying an unloaded and locked pistol is not unlawful, and thus your pistol shouldn't be any concern of his. You will *not* show him your pistol, nor will you get back in your car *until* your business is completed and he has gone.

I've never tried this, but it would *seem* to thwart any otherwise lawful order to return to your car (as such would, in this case, *increase* the cop's risks--not reduce them). Any readers with the guts to try this and report back, will have their experiences discussed in any 2nd edition of *You & The Police!*

Another incident worked out *better* because I *had* gotten out. **Boston's real-life incident #2:** I was on the highway doing about 75 mph and gradually overtook a trashed out pickup. "Hardass" got his stupid ego involved, passed me and then resumed his 65 mph. I kept my speed constant and passed him. When he passed me *again,* I got tired of the cat and mouse, flew by, outdistancing him by a mile when a highway patrolman (hiding beyond an overpass) zapped me at 80mph.

I pulled over rather quickly and got out just as he had stopped. The junker pickup roared past just as the HP and I met. HP's eyes bugged out at the sight of my holstered pistol (open carry was lawful in that state). I calmly admitted to speeding and explained that it was to outdistance the weird guy in the beatup truck. I further explained that his license plate was attached in a suspicious manner, probably to make it hard to read. The HP, once presented with this reasonable story, took off! Though I was clean-cut and polite, I was armed and I think that he merely wanted to leave.

My girlfriend at the time was with me, and was astonished to see me return to the car after 20 seconds and the HP driving off. Though an good pistol shot herself, she was admittedly too *"squirmy"* to carry openly.

Your actions and body movements are crucial.

Make sure your hands move normally, and keep them seen at all times (out of your pockets). Relax and let your arms hang naturally. Crossed arms are a subliminal sign of defiance. Do *not* light up a cigarette, especially at night. Drunk drivers typically do this to hide their alcohol breath.

Be pleasant and find out *why* he stopped you.

This assumes you weren't stopped for doing 100 mph in a school-zone. If the reason is obvious, *don't ask* because you'll come off as a real smartass. On this point, the funniest example I ever saw was the opening 3 minutes of some TV show. A Porsche 928 led about 15 cops on a horrific high-speed chase all over L.A. When finally cornered in a parking garage, a cop guardedly approached the driver's tinted window. It rolled down to expose a very distinguished older gentleman in an expensive suit, with a beautiful young lady. Utterly smooth, he asked, *"Is there a problem, Officer?"*

If suspicious, cops don't like to immediately tell you why they stopped you. What you don't know is leverage against you, and they are loath to give up that leverage. You must quickly find out why you've been stopped to understand how The Scene is likely to play.

I don't care much for the tired, old line, *"Is there a problem, Officer?"* Try something totally disarming and innocuous: *"Did I do something wrong, Officer?"* The cop may blurt out the real reason for stopping you. If the nice, innocent approach doesn't work, then you'll probably have to be hardnosed. Give nothing until he shows a bit of courtesy and explains. You might have to be pretty insistent here.

Once you know, defuse his suspicion and seek to leave. Once you've offered a perfectly reasonable explanation for your behavior, you've pretty much terminated the basis for detention. You're now on the higher ground. Don't budge by answering more questions. Keep seeking to leave. (If you don't, remaining *could* appear voluntary.)

Don't be in an obvious hurry to get out of there.

Gushing relief and thanks is only suspicious to a cop--it makes him wonder what he *really* missed. Save the rejoicing for later. On the flip side, don't *overdo* the "ain't-no-thing" bit. Once released, don't hang around and make conversation, figuring you're in clear so why not "rap with the Man." *Slide on outta there!* You're not safe until you're gone.

"NO, YOU'RE NOT FREE TO GO!"

Once your paperwork has been returned with his lecture or ticket (or both), you're free to go unless he has additional RAS to detain you further. **If this happens, be *extremely* on guard.** For some reason, you're likely on a short, slippery rope to arrest. I've got a couple of stories:

Boston's real-life incident #3:

I was on a road trip (a working vacation with research materials and computer to write *Good-Bye April 15th!*). The day had not started well; I had overslept an early morning departure, missed breakfast, and was running very late for a meeting 300 miles away. And then I got nabbed on the highway for 75+ mph, just a half hour from my destination. That capped off an already rotten morning. The cop routinely wrote up my ticket, handed it to me with my license and matter-of-factly asked if he could look in my trunk.

Me: (Coldly:) *"No, you may not. I don't have time for it, and there's nothing inside to concern you."*

Cop: *"It'll only take a minute."*

Me: (Annoyed:) *"I don't have 'a minute.' I'm late already, which is why I was speeding, remember? I need to be on my way now."*

Cop: *"No, stay right here. You appear nervous to me, and I think you're hiding something."* (Even though this was insufficient basis for RAS, he claimed he had RAS, so I had to remain.)

Me: (Extremely annoyed:) *"I'm not nervous! I'm just tired, hungry, and I don't like speeding tickets, much less being treated like a criminal."*

Cop: (Unmoved:) *"Just stay here, I'll be right back."* (He then went back to his car, and returned after being on the radio for a good 5 minutes.) *"O.K., here's the deal. You know and I know that I can't search* *your trunk without either your permission or probable cause. So, what I've done is call for the drug dog, and if he alerts to the presence of drugs that gives me probable cause, and I will search your car."*

Me: (Coolly angry:) *"I wish I could say that you're 'barking up the wrong tree,' but you're not even barking up a 'tree!' Taking drugs to ____* (a major "drug source city") *is like taking french fries to MacDonalds! It's ridiculous! Since you've pushed this so far, I'm going to get my camcorder and film this whole thing."* (This was during the uproar over Rodney King's beating.)

Cop: (Going absolutely ballistic:) *"You will not film this, you will not record this! I'm in control of this scene!"*

As I didn't then know my legal grounds on this point, I acquiesced. What I've since learned is that as long as you don't interfere with their duties, you've got a perfect right to video The Scene. Heck, if the police get to have TV's *Cops* film the Scenes, why can't you?

Anyway, after only 5 minutes a deputy arrived with his dog. He and the cop huddled for a moment, and then the deputy walked over leading his dog. He started at my driver's door and ambled back to the trunk, subtly touching the lid along the way. (This is clever and shabby trick. What they do is first touch a bag of pot in their pocket, then slyly transfer the scent onto whatever they want the dog to "alert." It's guaranteed to create probable cause.) Predictably, the dog alerted to my trunk.

Cop: (Smugly:) *"Did you see that? He alerted to the presence of drugs in your trunk. I now have probable cause to search it. Open it."*

Me: *"Nice trick. Well, you all may have just concocted probable cause, but I don't have to help you in this. I will not open my trunk, as such may be construed as consent."*

Cop: (Giving me a pretextual *Terry* frisk to find the trunk key:) *"Now you're not under arrest here, I'm just patting you down for weapons."*

About this time (without a second radio call, thus confirming my suspicions of a setup) a DEA agent drove up, drooling over another prospect. He was a stunningly obese 300 pounder, sweating more than Charles Laughton in a sauna. The three of them emptied out my packed trunk (mainly full of books, which caused them some bafflement). After conferring with the other two cops, he sauntered over and tried to "Good Cop" me (like I've got the I.Q. of salad).

DEA: *"Howya doin? So, you like camping?"* (I had gear in the car.)
Me: (Bored:) *"Don't talk to me like I'm some hick at a bar."* (He asked some more questions which I either ignored or deflected.)
DEA: (Angrily:) *"Well, you won't cooperate! You're just an ✱sshole!"*
Me: (Icily:)   *"I was under the impression that your agency had standards for language and* (looking at his big beer gut) *physical fitness."*

With that he stomped off. By now, my whole trunk's contents had been emptied and laid out behind my car in two rows, with the dog doing a figure eight through them. He alerted to nothing. Frustrated, they had the dog jump in the trunk, and he didn't alert to the empty trunk, *either.*   Now, *really* frustrated, they started pawing through my bags (even though they did not have *specific* PC to search through any of them).

Not finding anything, they opened my passenger door (*without* the dog having first alerted to the passenger interior). The dog leapt in over my color monitor and kicked it out with his hind legs, sending it rolling down the shoulder. He then tore around my front seat and dash, trashing it with his muddy paws and breaking an expensive pair of sunglasses. The back seat was piled to the ceiling, so he couldn't get back there. Since his actions were inconclusive, they called for a *second* dog.

It arrived with the county sheriff himself, leisurely climbed on the front seat and proceeded to have a nap. Now, the four cops and two dogs are looking pretty stupid. It's become a "status/penis thing" and they're now *really* intent on finding some drugs in my car to justify the whole thing. This is where I got concerned that they would plant some. (Don't get your sensibilities in a pinch; cops plant stuff if they're desperate.)

Me: *"This has obviously been a mistake, and I think even you realize it by now. As I said, I've nothing to do with drugs. The only drugs that could be found in my car are those that were put there."*

They didn't like this at all, and proceeded to empty out the interior, pull up the back seat, open the hood to look in the air cleaner--the works. Traffic is now diverted around us because of 80 feet of orange pylons behind us. It's a Scene.

To illustrate how incompetent these guys were, listen to this: They found my pistol (which was lawfully owned and carried), cleared the chamber, called in the serial number, set the pistol on top of a bag not four feet away, *turned their backs on me and went back to going through my car!* Had they done this to the wrong guy, he could have easily grabbed the pistol, hit the slide release and gunned them down! These were *sloppy* cops.

So, they've gone through the entire car and all my bags, finding zip. I'm disgusted and the look on my face is one would have after catching some pervert masturbating in the park. Without a word, they began putting the stuff back in my car.

Me: (Disgustedly:)   *"'Thank you,' but I'll do that! I think you've handled my things enough for today."*

I packed it all back up and walked over to them, sullenly congregating like the jackals they were.

Me: *"Well, had enough? Am I free to go now?"*
Cop: (Flatly:)   *"Yes."*

Me : (Outraged:) *"'Yes?' That's all you've got to say after all this? No, 'Our mistake--we apologize.'? No 'Sorry for breaking your stuff and wasting 45 minutes of your time, Sir."?"*
Cop: (Suddenly indignant:) *"Hey, we're just doing our job!"* (Ah, the old "Nuremberg defense!")
Me: *"Hah! Gentlemen, <u>before</u> this incident I thought pretty highly of the police. Now, I <u>don't</u>. You're squandering the very thing you need--the good faith obedience of the American people. Honest folks aren't going to take this crap forever, and someday you'll be in for a rude awakening! Go catch some <u>criminals</u> and leave the rest of us <u>alone</u>!*

On a happy note, I contested the ticket and demanded a jury trial. Word got around the courthouse that I was pretty hot and that a civil suit was likely. They dropped the matter. So, no fine *and* I got an educational experience from it all. *Heh!* Did I do anything about this outrage later? No. Except to write this book. That's the best justice for hyenas like them.

... THE LOCAL NEWSPAPER, JUDGE, PASTOR, COMMISSIONERS, GOVERNOR, POLICE CHIEF ——*DO IT*-- OR SHUT UP, SHEEP !!

What would I do differently today? A few things. I would have embarked on the road in a better frame of mind. I would have been more alert and probably avoided being nabbed for speeding. I would have forbidden the dog handler to touch my car. I would have indeed camcorded the search. I would have gotten everyone's' name and badge number. I would have filed a lawsuit for a groundless detention. Generally, I would have raised a real stink. They had *their* fun, so why not have *mine?*

Are you ready for another *"No, you're not free to go"* story?

Boston's real-life incident #4:

Late at night I was stopped for speeding by a highway patrolman (HP). In my experience, minority cops more often have a "chip on their shoulders" and this guy (an Hispanic) didn't "disappoint." He was very near to being a Rogue Cop.

While I tried to located my license in my wallet, he got impatient after about 5 seconds, exclaimed, *"Give me that!"* and grabbed for my wallet! I won the brief tug-of-war, and from then on both of us were pretty angry. He then asked to search my motorcycle saddlebags (which were locked).

Upon indignantly refusing, he tried to open them himself, but couldn't. Tapping on each bag, he commented that one seemed empty but the other didn't. (So *what!*) To him, that seemed suspicious, and he again demanded that I open the "full" bag. I refused.

By this time, two other HP units had responded--who knows what the first HP claimed on the radio. He and another HP conferred *in my very presence* about coming up with some pretext to impound the bike so they could search it. My attitude grew quite hostile at that point and I snidely quipped that, *"You two were born about fifty years too late--the Führer could have used a couple of more guys like you!"* (Not recommended...)

Things *really* went downhill at that, and the third HP (a fairly reasonable guy, as it turned out) interceded, *"You have a really poor attitude! Have you had bad experiences with the police?"* He seemed genuinely concerned, so I replied, *"No, but I'm having one right now with him!"* (pointing to the HP who stopped me). *"Unless you can talk some sense into him, he's going to make a career mistake here and drag you two guys down with him."* That had the desired effect, so Nice HP took the first HP behind his car and calmed him down.

He returned, handed me my ticket, and the other guys drove off. While putting my gear back on, he honked and motioned me back to his car. *"Uh, oh,"* I mused; he's going to get me back there and concoct some story about me attacking him or something--anything to arrest me and impound the bike. *Very* warily, I approached his passenger window. He told me to get in and I understandably refused. He realized why I was suspicious and explained that he had made a mistake on my ticket. (HP's often cover several jurisdictions, and he had written the wrong court on my ticket.) He merely wanted to correct it, so I allowed him to do so, and he drove off.

Still smelling a rat, that he was trying send me to the *wrong* court (the "corrected" one), I sent Not Guilty pleas to *both* courts with an explanation. Happily, the HP's ticket somehow got *lost* between courts and nobody ever contacted me! *Heh!*

"Would you mind if I searched your...?"

Cops routinely ask to search, even when they really aren't all that suspicious. They know that it never hurts to ask. Don't get all weak-kneed if this happens to you. Use some verbal judo:

You: (Flatly:) *"What would you be searching for?"*
Cop: *"Well, drugs."* (Sometimes it's for guns.)
You: (Coolly:) *"Why don't you first ask me if I had such in my car?"*

This politely shames the cop, and makes him look coarse and illmannered. Nobody ever speaks to cops this way, especially criminals. The cop will be knocked off track and likely become flustered over his embarrassment. He'll now get tougher:

Cop: (Impatiently:) *"Well, if you've nothing to hide you shouldn't object to a search, should you?"*
You: (Lightly:) *"What a tired fig leaf that old line is! Have you ever thought of applying such 'reasoning' to your own property?"*
Cop: (Angrily:) *"So, you're refusing to cooperate?"*
You: (Patiently:) *"I don't believe in wasting my time or tax dollars by agreeing to pointless searches. If you really had PC you could have searched without my consent. Since you obviously don't have PC, I'll be*

on my way before you jeopardize your career any further. There are crim-inals out there to be caught, and being here with me is <u>not</u> the best use of your time. Good day, Officer."

The cop will realize that you're the wrong guy to push about, and will make as face-saving retreat as he can. (Or else he will try to *kill* you...) Granted, this kind of talk takes courage, but it's occasionally necessary.

- 14 -

TALKING YOUR WAY OUT
OF TICKETS

Some people are able to talk their way out of tickets, but most aren't. It seems to be more an inherent talent than a teachable one, however, I will show you at least the basics.

If you're stopped for speeding, etc.

First of all, if he exits his patrol car *without* his ticket book, then you've got a very good chance of merely getting a lecture and not a ticket. This doesn't happen too often, so don't blow it. Allow him his spiel, be contrite, and apologize for your driving. No posterior kissing is necessary here, just play along with his scenario because it's to *your* advantage. Many cops have the same lecturing attitude as third-grade teachers, so let them posture a bit if it saves you a ticket.

If, however, he exits ticket book in hand, then you're likely to get written up. The only chance you'll have to talk your way out of a ticket entirely is to do it *before* he sets pen to pad. His tickets are precious revenue tools of the State, and he must account for each one. The odds of him ripping up a ticket are about the same as you putting Super Unleaded in a rental Yugo.

Some DON'Ts: *Don't* challenge, *don't* beg, *don't* threaten, *don't* cry, *don't* argue, *don't* get sarcastic, *don't* insinuate that the cop is lying or prejudiced against you, *don't* lie about some "emergency," *don't* rationalize, *don't* equivocate, *don't* whine and *don't* name drop.

David W. Kelly's *How To Talk Your Way Out Of A Traffic Ticket* (ISBN 0-918259-21-5) offers some good lines:

"I'm normally a safe driver, Officer, but for a second my attention was elsewhere. I promise I'll try to be more careful."

"Insurance for a person my age is quite high, so I have been trying to keep my record clean. Could you trust me to not make the same mistake again?"

"I have a perfect driving record. If you just give me a warning this time, I'll do my best to keep it that way."

"I didn't realize that was illegal. I wouldn't have done it if I had known. I certainly know now!"

"I know this situation is my own fault. Can you excuse me this time? I promise you won't have to stop me again."

"It has been a long drive. You just made me realize I need to stop and get some coffee."

"I'm new to this area, Officer. I guess I need to pay closer attention to my driving."

"I'm sorry, I should be paying closer attention. I'm upset over a personal situation and it's hard to concentrate on other things right now. But I promise I'll be more careful."

"Officer, is there something I can do or say that you will make a decision not to write a ticket this time and give me just a warning instead?"

You'll have only the first minute (or less) to talk your way out, as the cop must quickly decide whether or not to ticket you.

It didn't work--he's writing you up.

What you *might* be able to do is plead for a non-moving violation instead of a "mover." The State still gets its Ø (which is all the State *really* cares about, anyway) but your record will not be affected by a ticket for a broken headlight, etc. In my experience, you'll have a 1 in 4 chance of this, and you must go for it before he reaches the violation line on your ticket. Try it!

Don't make it worse.

Whatever the infraction, don't buy into a worse scene with a counterproductive attitude. Getting a ticket is bad enough. Keep The Scene at that level. It took me awhile to really learn this. Get legal satisfaction *later*, but your goal now is *leaving*.

Often, I'd get a totally bogus ticket and it really rankled me. Once, I was pulled over in an extremely flagrant speed trap and made a big stink about taking the thing to trial. Mistake. *Never* tell the cop that you even *might* dispute a ticket, for he'll simply tack on some additional baggage to the original infraction. Trust me on this. **Get your ticket and *go*.** (Now, I ask the cop how to send in payment, for I want him to *believe* that he's "made a sale." That way, he'll write fewer notes (if any) on the stop because of the little apparent chance of my disputing it.)

Save your "big guns" for the arraignment and trial, where you'll have the presumption of innocence in one of their overloaded courts. *There* is where your advantage will be.

Making the ticket go away.

You can either plead Not-Guilty and win in court (preferably in a *jury* trial), or the State may simply drop the case (through Defensive Driving Course, deferred adjudication, or a decline of prosecution). How firm you are depends on how much beating the ticket means to you. I've taken at least twenty tickets to trial, and the State dropped 1 in 3. (The others I usually won, or got a reduced fine. I say, "Go for it!" It's fun, educational and your odds are very good.)

- 15 -

YOUR HOUSE, JOB
& THE POLICE

Inside your house (and business, if nonpublic and unregulated) you have the most rights. There is no intermediate level of intrusion such as the *Terry* frisk. And, if arrested inside, there is no inventory search of the room (although a search incident to arrest still applies to areas within *"lunging distance."*)

The only legal way for the cops to come through your door *without* an exigency or your consent (both covered in Chapter 8 and assumed to be moot possibilities in your case) is via **arrest** already in progress from a public place, or a **warrant** (search or arrest). This chapter covers only those two avenues.

In view of that, coupled with the assumption that you are not a criminal, the chances of the police barging through your door are nearly nonexistent. There is, however, still the chance that someday the police will at least come to your house for questioning, and I'll show you how to handle that, too.

YOUR *"REASONABLE EXPECTATION OF PRIVACY"* WITHIN YOUR HOUSE

The 4th Amendment specifically protects your *"house"* from unwarranted police intrusions. The *"curtilage"* (or *"premises"*) around your house usually includes your garage/carport, a fenced-in backyard, and nearby buildings. Within your house and surrounding premises, you have a *"reasonable expectation of privacy."* Such 4th Amendment protection does not extend to the *"open fields"* around your *"premises/curtilage,"* nor to front yards, porches, driveways, or sidewalks.

Anything that can be seen/heard/smelled by a passerby (mailman, neighbor, salesman, etc.) without any extra effort is fair game for probable cause--though, a warrant is still necessary to gain entry.

"KNOCK, KNOCK -- IT'S THE COPS."

If the police come to your door to question you, *beware.* It's for *their* benefit, not yours. As I explained in Chapter 5, there is rarely any advantage to speaking with the police about your affairs. Help them catch criminals, but don't talk about yourself.

If you have information about a crime, either speak to them *through* a closed door (not window), or over the phone. **Do not allow them in your house.** While they may insist, cajole or even plead, *keep them outside*--one way or another. If such strikes them as suspicious, explain that the house is not tidied up for guests, or that everybody has the flu, whatever.

If you've reported an incident in your house and the police are there to investigate, make sure you've locked up all irrelevant areas and sensitive items (guns, papers, cash, etc.). If the entire house seems within investigative scope, lock up the stuff in your car (parked in your driveway, not on the street). Do not allow them to wander about unaccompanied. When their job is done, politely escort them out. Be cordial, but not overly friendly. Remember, they don't work for you, they work for the *State*--and you know what the State is in search of...

HOW TO ARREST IN A HOUSE

The Suspect's House

No amount of PC, even 100% certainty that the evidence or "wanted" person is inside his house, will justify a warrantless entry. (Not *yet*, anyway...)

A warrant is only necessary if the subject or evidence is *already inside* the house/curtilage. If the cops have PC (though no warrant) to arrest you, and they see you in your front yard, on your porch, or even inside your house behind the front door cracked open--they may proceed to come inside your house since the arrest began in a "public" place. As ruled in **U.S. v. Santana**, 427 US 38, 42-43 (1976), *"a suspect may not defeat an arrest which has been set in motion in a public place...by the expedient of escaping to a private place."*

Practical tips.

If you believe the police have PC (though not yet a warrant) to arrest, stay in your house, and do not open the door. Draw all curtains. Do *not* answer the door or phone, as such will give the cops PC to believe that you're inside.

If you believe that a warrant *is* imminent, then you obviously do *not* want to be arrested *inside* your house.

Stay outside your house and car. If you are picked up, you want it to occur as a pedestrian in public. You want to keep the police outside your property, if possible. (If, however, they have a *search* warrant, then tough--the police *will* gain lawful entry.)

Unless you want to hide out, perhaps the best thing to do is voluntarily appear with your lawyer. Such will look very good to the court and DA, save yourself a lot of pre-arrest worry, *and* keep the police out of your house.

For those, however, who cannot bring themselves to simply give up to the police, yet cannot stay in their house, one solid option exists: leave the jurisdiction and hole up in a hotel (paid with cash), or a third party's house. I mention this, not to assist real criminals, but to assist those who might become victim to a baseless or politically-motivated action. The government's hands are rarely clean, and one might someday fall under undue persecution.

A Third Party's House

In order to enter a third party's house (where the arrestee is not domiciled) a cop must have a *search* warrant (unless consent or exigency is present) according to ***Stegald v. United States***, 451 US 254 (1981). Assuming there's no PC to search the third party's house, the police cannot obtain a search warrant ever as a pretext to arrest a subject.

Make sure this friend will not give you up, and has a cool, unflappable demeanor. Do not use his phone or expose yourself to view. Do not tell *anybody* of your location--not even your lawyer, unless he assures you of attorney-client relationship and his mandated silence. Even then, I'd hesitate revealing your location.

WHEN THEY HAVE A WARRANT

Search Warrant only.

The warrant should be specific and accurate. *"Premises"* is broader than *"house"* and they cannot search beyond the scope stated in the warrant. Try very hard to see and read the warrant yourself during (if not before) the search. If they have utterly the wrong address, tell them and firmly demand that they leave at once. If they refuse, demand immediate "judicial review" by the court. Refusal exhibits "bad faith" on their part and should nullify the warrant, if not get you some damages in a lawsuit.

You will not be arrested immediately unless they find contraband. You and others *will,* however, be detained inside (***Michigan v. Summers***, 452 US 692 (1981)). Visitors who cannot be immediately tied to crime-related activity should not be detained further, much less arrested.

Try to camcord the search. Expect improper search procedures, abusive behavior, and even planted evidence. The cops will try to forbid the filming, but as long as you're not interfering with a lawful search, they have no legal right to stop you. Admit nothing--in fact, say nothing.

Arrest Warrant only.

If the police knock and announce that they have an arrest warrant for you, reply that you are unarmed and are coming out. Empty all your pockets, and seek to leave through an unguarded exit, lock it behind you, and meet them with your hands held high. **You want them to arrest you *outside* your house, if possible.** Doing so will lessen your *"grabbable reach"* and thus the scope of the *"search incident to lawful arrest."* Wherever they first see you, that's where they get to search. The best place for them to arrest you is in your backyard, which is semi-private, yet outside.

They might have the back door covered, so pick another exit without making it look like you're trying to flee. If you open the front door, they will enter and arrest you inside. So, think in advance of the optimum exit. In the foyer, or kitchen back door is probably best.

If arrested *inside,* the police can usually make a *"protective sweep"* of the entire premises (not just *"grabbable reach"*) to search for dangerous persons. During such a sweep, they cannot search in places incapable of concealing a person, such as small containers. These sweeps are also much harder to justify if the arrest takes place outside, though not impossible.

Both Search *and* Arrest Warrants.

You got problems. First, you will be arrested, and second, they get to come inside and ransack your house. You'll have no freedom to camcord the search, or even tape-record the arrest (though others present might).

No-Knock Warrants.

Usually the police must knock-announce-wait during the execution of a warrant. The exceptions to this requirement are:

❐ The warrant expressly authorizes forcible entry without prior announcement. The cop's affidavit must state specific explainable reasons why he cannot knock and announce, or,

❐ Circumstances known to the cop *after* the warrant's issue give him PC to believe that notice prior entry is likely:

➊ to result in the easy destruction/disposal of evidence; or
➋ to endanger one's life or safety; or
➌ to enable suspect to escape; or
➍ a "useless gesture" as those inside know why the police are there and will not respond, or the cop *knows* no one is inside.

Allegedly, it is very difficult for the cops to convince a court *ex post facto* that these exceptional difficulties existed.

"Best" yet, even if they are required to knock and announce, they have to wait only a *"reasonable"* amount of time before entering if the dweller delays or refuses to answer the door. What is a *"reasonable"* time length? ***U.S. v. Cruz***, 265 F.Supp 15, 23-24 (W.D. Tex. 1967) ruled **15 seconds!** Great.

AH, SWEET PRIVACY!

In my case, there is not a scrap of paper to link me to my house I have no phone, utility, rent, or mortgage records in my name. No license, credit card, or bill has my house location on it. *Nada.* In today's atmosphere, full of snoops, nosy do-gooders, bloodthirsty collection agencies, litigious leeches, and an increasingly militarized police, it makes no sense to be easily located.

While I realize that this sounds "paranoid" to most of you, think of the advantages: your assets are generally safe from lawsuits, credit hounds cannot bang at your door, you can't be arrested in your pajamas for some old speeding ticket, "old friends" cannot drop by because they "just happened to be in the neighborhood," old romances cannot disturb you, etc.

Such is easy to arrange, too. Using a street addressed (not a P.O. Box) mail receiving service ("A") as your "home address" you can then rent/own a domicile elsewhere (preferably in another name). The mail drop, which unknowingly has *another* mail drop address ("B") as your "real" address (and vice-versa) receives all your mail and bills. Your real home is free of all that and the related headaches. Your public phone number is merely a voice mail, while your home phone is established in another name.

I have lived like this for many years. The catalyst for all this was nearly being arrested at my doorstep for an old speeding ticket (which had been paid, but the record lost by computer). Though eventually sorted out, I resolved never to allow it happen again.

Years later, because of these prior arrangements, I easily avoided being subpoenaed for an utterly baseless Ø800 civil suit filed by a money-grubbing pest (and full-time cretin). The paper-serving deputy simply couldn't find me, so the pest had no choice but to glomm onto somebody else.

I also avoided the constant nuisance of an remarkably unbalanced woman who, being desperately unhappy with her marriage, developed an unprovoked fixation on me (a platonic friend), almost to the point of a "fatal attraction." She was quite ingenious and persistent in her efforts to find me, going to such lengths as to even call my family impersonating credit card representatives and hospital staff. While she fooled a few people and managed to wheedle bits of information, she never found out where I lived or worked. After months of trying, she finally gave up and became fixated on someone else.

Finally, these arrangements have allowed me, pseudo-nymously, to write material critical of oppressive government and helpful to liberty-minded folks. While *anybody* can be located with enough time and expense, I am simply not *worth* such effort--which is fine by me.

I yearn for a polite and respectful world where I could have a listed phone number in my own name without concern of being bothered, but it ain't gonna happen any time soon. Even though I'm a dreamer and an optimist, I'm a realist, *first.* Privacy is like fire insurance; you can't get it *after* you need it. You get it first, and then hope that it never becomes necessary.

The December 1995 issue of *The McAlvany Intelligence Advisor* is all about privacy. To order (or better yet, subscribe) call 1-800-528-0559. I very highly recommend the *MIA.*

One last thing: **Don't be *obvious* about your privacy.** Folks will quickly get suspicious if you seem evasive, nonresponsive, cagey, or untruthful.   Give enough harmless information to quench their curiosity and you'll generally find them satisfied. (People really aren't *that* intelligent these days, and *rarely* will you meet the shrewd soul who discerns your answers to be a bit thin.)   Most people live on the most superficial of levels, and a veneer of information is all they will desire (or can handle). Have your "veneer" down pat.

Nothing casts suspicion more than somebody *not* having a phone number and street address.   Get a separate voice mail number which sounds like an answering machine, and a street addressed mail receiving service. Then, superficially at least, you'll seem just like everybody else--and that's all they care about, anyway.

- 16 -

OUR DWINDLING RIGHTS

I wish that our effective rights, whittled away as they are, could yet remain *in stasis*. Such is pipe dream. The onslaught continues. This book may very well end up a small, bitter slice of legal nostalgia by 2005, if not sooner.

JUDICIAL TYRANNY

The federal courts, especially the Supreme Court, has actively removed many Constitutional safeguards, the most notable being your right to a trial by jury in all criminal trials. In a horrific bit of *Animal Farm* "except for" jurisprudence (***Blanton v. North Las Vegas***, 489 US 541), the Supreme Court ruled that offenses carrying less than six months imprisonment are deemed *"petty offenses"* in which the 6th Amendment right to jury trials is *inapplicable*. Funny, I don't recall the 6th Amendment mentioning *"petty offenses:"*

In ALL criminal prosecutions, the accused shall enjoy the right to a speedy and public trial, by an impartial jury... (my emphasis)

When *"all"* can mean "some," the handwriting is on the wall.

Blanton doctrine was upheld in early 1993 when a drunk driver in Yosemite National Park was denied a jury trial, and sued the Government. The Supreme Court ruled 9-0 (***U.S. v. Nachtigal***, 113 S.Ct. 1072) that there is *no* constitutional right to a jury trial for drunk driving committed on federal territory (a *"petty offense"*). This was no disputable point of law--the Court ruled *unanimously*. ("Home of the free," indeed!)

And now for some good news. My personal feeling is that, from here on out, fewer *new* inroads will be made on liberty through the courts. Though outright reversals are too much to hope for, what we are beginning to see in court rulings is a brake on *additional* government encroachment on freedom. Case in point: the 1995 ***Lopez*** ruling which perhaps dawns the end of unlimited federal commerce clause expansion.

Also, the police have plenty of judicial circumventions around the 4th Amendment based on the tired fig leaf of *"reasonableness"* and even liberal courts seem reluctant to add more. Congress, however, will not be so stingy.

CONGRESSIONAL TYRANNY

Much of the Federal Government's expansion has been accomplished through Congressional application of their Constitutional treaty power (VI:2) and the interstate commerce clause (I:8:3). These two "wild card" powers allow Congress to circumvent any and all Constitutional restrictions. (My next book will cover this in shocking detail. Stay tuned...)

Congress has gotten so bold that it doesn't even resort to its "wild cards" anymore. Case in point: H.R. 666.

House Resolution 666

The "exclusionary rule" is loathed by the government, and is under full attack by H.R. 666 (not enumerated in the AP wire story, for obvious reasons!), the so-called *Exclusionary Rule Reform Act of 1994.* Such would, in *federal* cases, abolish the historical requirement of a warrant prior to entry of your house Kick-down doors, warrantless searches/arrests (and their resulting evidence, normally the *"fruit of the poisoned tree"*) would be upheld if the feds claim such were in *"good faith"* compliance with the 4th Amendment. Since Congress cannot unilaterally get rid of the 4th, Congress proposes to allow the federal stormtroopers to merely pay "lip service" to it!

The state of political/legal ignorance is such that this ludicrous proposition is pretty much swallowed whole. When the legislature may, at its pleasure, so basely abrogate its operating charter because of a bovine, feeding-at-the-public-trough constituency, liberty is clearly on its deathbed.

We *can* halt this, however. You need to spread the word about a concept once discussed in civics classes: **Congress cannot, on its own, render void the Constitution.** For if it can, as the 1933 German parliament bypassed the Weimar Constitution after the Nazi-staged Reichstag fire, then we are on a short road to fascism. (Read *The Ominous Parallels* by Leonard Peikoff.)

EXECUTIVE ORDERS / MARTIAL LAW

When the gradual methods don't work, the State becomes desperate and sloughs off all facades of legality. This is called martial law. The people become, finally, utter subjects to the executive authority. This *can* happen *here*.

If it *does*, then this little book will serve only as a bitter reminder to the marginal freedom we once enjoyed. You can tell your children, *"In my day, back in '96, we'd demand the police to state their 'reasonable suspicion' and they'd back off!"*

The supposition of this book is--that with adequate numbers of courageous folks, newly trained in the basics of Constitutional law--we can grind to a halt further encroachments of our Liberty. When a great weight is pressing upon you, it must first be stopped before it can be cast off. *You & The Police!* is about stopping the weight. Casting it off is another story for other books, such as my *Good-Bye April 15th!*

This weight of tyranny, even *slightly* further pressed against us, will materialize as martial law. I'm talking price controls, curfews, currency exchange restrictions, equity transfer moratoriums, a new incontrovertible "dollar," mandatory civil service, roadblock checkpoints, etc. When the President says, *"Jump!"* you'll reply, *"Yes, Sir!--how high?"*

It *can* happen here. If Hitler happened in the land of Bach and Goethe, tyranny can happen in America.

This martial law will be based on the 1917 *Trading With The Enemy Act* and similar wartime acts of WWII and Korea. We've been in a state of "national emergency" since at least

1933, and maybe even since 1917. **More shocking still, the roots for this lie in the *Constitution itself*,** which allows (in I:9:2) the suspension of at least the *"privilege of the writ of habeas corpus...when in cases...the public safety may require it."* Our state of "national emergency" has never been rescinded, to my knowledge. (Read Dr. Eugene Schroder's *The Constitution: Fact Or Fiction.* ISBN 1-885534-06-X)

AMERICA'S FUTURE

Oh, it "can't happen in *America?"* The assertion contains its own rebuttal: it *will* happen here precisely because nobody believes it possible. History seems to love ironies, and the greatest irony imaginable is that *the most free nation ever in human record* could become the most totalitarian. America has a deep nosy, puritanical streak which is just the kind of fertile "spy-on-your-neighbor" soil necessary to an empowered State. There are millions of pious left-lane loiterers who literally *delight* in slowing down highway traffic to the silly speed limit.

> *The battle for personal liberty seems to have been attained,* **but in the absence of the din and clash, we cannot comprehend the meaning of the safeguards employed...** *The oppression of the crowns and principalities is unquestionably over,* **and merciless majorities may yet constitute one of the chapters of future history** [of new and vicious oppression].
>   *U.S. v. James,* 60 F. 264, at 265 (1894)

"Can't happen here"--*Ha!* I can't envision it happening anywhere *else.* Practically every other nation has gone through this, and given our patent lack of "vaccinations" we're long overdue for some *real* tyranny.

It is *so* close to happening here because the entire country is dead asleep in a drunken stupor of materialism, apathy and gutlessness. Congress proposed to abolish the 4th Amendment, even titling the thing in demonic fashion as H.R. 666, and everybody remained inexorably glued to the O.J. trial.

I sometime wonder why I even *bother.* So, why *do* I bother? With my training and experience in international finance I could be easily drawing 6 figures. I bother, first, because I *care.* And, I bother, secondly, because something I write *may* make a difference. (Thank God for desktop publishing! My small voice can actually reach the interested minority.)

I am metaphorically driven by a Dr. Seuss story called *Horton Hears A Who.* A microscopic planet faces destruction unless the inhabitants make enough noise to attract the attention of their big-eared elephant friend, Horton. Their whole world is in the streets, making a howling racket, yet it's not enough. A small boy is found, alone in his apartment, silently bouncing his yo-yo. Entreated to at least make some sort of sound, he manages a puny *"Yopp!"* Sonically, it is the *"drop which overflowed the vase,"* as the French would say. Horton at last hears the tiny planet and rescues it.

You or I *could* be that small boy. I do not want to live a fat, comfortable, self-serving life--when I *could* have been that *"drop which overflowed the vase."* We can never know *what* effect we have (or *could* have had) on the human outcome. As foolish or frantic as my activities may seem, I will at least not have cloistered myself away, exercising my yo-yo. Hence, I fight against H.R. 666 and its ilk. I just don't know any better.

CORRECTING THE MODERN BULLY

Our most likely brush with the State is the traffic stop. It is clear that the 55/65 mph speed limit (a result of both Congressional extortion and timidity amongst the State governors) and its demanded enforcement was the initial catalyst in the tragic transformation of our police (from reasonable peace officer to the modern revenue-based "law enforcement" officer).

The State cannot afford, financially or legally, to roust *everyone*, so it must randomly flex its muscle on the passersby in a sort of "negative lottery." While on the road or going through airports and checkpoints, you are vulnerable to this spotty attention. *"Your papers!"* is the common "greeting," followed by a general probe of your activities. We must squash this East German attitude.

Since we've allowed such intrusion on the streets, it has now seeped into our private and business affairs. We've but a few years to chasten this nosy bully, while he is still theoretically correctable. Some say that it's already too late, and they may indeed be correct regarding larger cities. Big Brother is a well-established cosmopolitan dude, but he is still weak in the countryside and must rely upon the local *gendarmes*--many of whom are still real peace officers.

The State hates an *armed* citizenry

The State, no longer content with its *raison d'etre* of merely keeping the peace, has abandoned its prime directive for one of social engineering. Incensed that some folks actually refuse allegiance to the "United Socialist States of America," the U.S.S.A. is now zealously swatting down us "cancerous cells." The State is especially hysterical over our "obsession" with guns. We are not "obsessed" with guns, but with freedom. Guns are simply the *means* to freedom. On this point, I also have ample experience.

Pack 'em if you got 'em!

I've occasionally attracted the State's attention by exercising my right (where permitted) to openly wear a sidearm. Though perfectly lawful in about twelve states, it is nonetheless relatively uncommon. I am not extraordinarily concerned with my personal safety, as I spend little time in high crime areas. So why *do* I wear a pistol? **To keep my rights *limber*.** To remind police and citizenry alike that I am still comparatively free and that I will act accordingly.

Granted, such *is* unusual and draws attention. This conspicuous attention is more properly imposed *inversely*--on the unarmed populace. When Emerson asked Thoreau (jailed for his tax protest against the Mexican-American War) why he was there, Thoreau gave the immortal reply, *"Why aren't you here?"* Thus, instead of *"Why are you armed?"* it should be, *"Why are the rest of you underlineunarmed?"*

If I could lawfully *conceal* carry without having to beg for Official Permission via an insulting permit card, I'd do so. On that point, you Vermonters are *truly* blessed. Let's see Handgun Control, Inc. explain why Vermont, with *no* restrictions on carrying, has virtually *no* violent crime!

Sadly, I have twice been accosted by cops for no other reason than my lawfully carried sidearm. While such hotheadedness is fairly rare, many (and maybe *most*) cops erroneously view gun-wearing as solely within *their* right. They can get real snitty when a "civilian" takes the 2nd Amendment at its word and has the *nerve* to actually "bear arms." This is ample evidence of how police mentality has inverted during the 1900's. Our supposed servants *believe* to be our masters, which is accepted by millions of "sheeple."

Attitude is the vital thing!

My personal philosophy is that one must constantly, without hurting others, seek the true boundaries and probe them. Find out where they are and see if they may be stretched. Life itself is a vast orchard of opportunity, yet 95% of people are self-incarcerated within their own mental hologram of desert corrals. *Everything* **begins with, and thus ultimately rests upon, only** *one* **thing: your** *vision.* See life as a desert corral, and a hot, dry, sandy, fly-ridden existence will be your reward. Instead of whining that others enjoy tropical fruit, why not see this life as the paradise it *can* be and get your *own* mangos?

What's my point? Don't allow others, *especially* the petty rule-makers and their bulldogs, to define or color your vision. There is Freedom to be had! Great pressures are in league to squeeze your Life and your Liberty into their manila folder for some bureaucratic filing cabinet--*resist!* **Get** *scrappy!* A lack of information isn't the problem; a lack of *guts* is. Fight for your life! I realize it's like sweeping water uphill and you'll have little help, but the only alternative is the deluge. Grab a "broom" and get back to sweeping!

I didn't write this book for the "sheeple." You know, those who bleat, *"If you've got nothing to hide, then you shouldn't object to a search of your stuff."* I wrote this book for you Americans who are horrified at the thought of warrantless searches of your property. I wrote it for the courageous who have properly armed themselves to protect their families amidst our savage society, regardless if such is technically illegal. (*"I'd rather be tried by twelve than carried by six."*)

Only *armed* **people can be** *free* **people, and the State knows this. We must first be** *disarmed* **in order to be** *enslaved.* This is an irrefutable historical constant. Every genocide in modern times was preceded by gun registration and confiscation. Much of the State's *future* oppression must and will deal with the coercive disarmament of individual

Americans, face to face. Such will require a "National Emergency" ("terrorist" or a "crime wave") and subsequent legislation. *Then* there will be Troops-In-Your-Street.

We still have time to exercise Liberty

Overt martial law is probably imminent, but not for a few years. The State must first, within the police and military, weed out those who cherish Liberty amongst the indoctrinated automata of enforcement (e.g., the Would-You-Shoot-An-American-Gunowner survey given to U.S. Marines at 29 Palms. In the meantime, we still enjoy a bit of breathing room.

The State must oppress within a framework of *perceived* law and justice, for if it doesn't, the State will lose its vital popular support. Within this perceived law and justice, you and I still have some good cards on our side. Right now, the State can only win through our own ignorance and fear. Our hand is still strong enough to make the State "fold" in a one-on-one game. Quit *believing* that the State always holds the winning hand. Learn your cards, and play them.

I'm not terribly enthusiastic about the *immediate* prognosis for Liberty, though I'm a hopeless optimist in the long run. Churchill once remarked, *"A lie is halfway around the world before truth even puts its boots on."* Truth and righteousness are marathoners, while evil sprints. The sprinters always lose their wind. This is a race between the Tortoise and the Hare. **We are witnessing the *last* sprint of the Hare.** He will plot and cheat and will seemingly have the Tortoise beat, but he will lose. He always *has*.

Keep a *long* perspective. This book will help you survive the short term. **Use wisdom and exercise courage.** The ugly Weed of Tyranny is growing strong in our national garden. **Our *fear* is its *water*.** Begin to no longer fear. Let's starve out this Weed while we *can*, or else the Flower of Freedom will be strangled from our land. Begin to no longer fear. Let's quit daydreaming about Liberty and start *living* it! **No more *fear!***

HOW TO ORDER FROM US

NOTE: The Ø symbol denotes "Federal Reserve Notes" which are no longer redeemable in, and masquerade as, real $ gold or silver money.

Good-Bye April 15th!
8½"x11", 392 pages. Published Nov. 1992. **Reprinted January 1999!**
Prices each: *1-3* copies are Ø40; *4-9* copies are Ø32; *10-15* copies are Ø24; a case of *16* or more copies are Ø20 each; 3 cases (48 copies) or more are Ø18.
S&H this book only: Book Rate add Ø4 first copy, and 50¢ each additional. Priority Mail/UPS: Ø5 first, Ø1 each additional copy thereafter.

You & The Police!
5½"x8½", 128 pages. Published January 1996.
Prices each: *1-5* copies are Ø15; *6-31* copies are Ø9; *32-91* copies are Ø8.40; a case of *92* or more copies are Ø7.50 each.

Bulletproof Privacy
5½"x8½", 160 pages. Published January 1997.
Prices each: *1-5* copies are Ø16; *6-31* copies are Ø10; *32-79* copies are Ø9; a case of *80* or more copies are Ø8 each.

Hologram of Liberty
5½"x8½", 262 pages. Published August 1997.
Prices each: *1-5* copies are Ø20; *6-15* copies are Ø12; *16-39* copies are Ø11.20; a case of *40* or more copies are Ø10 each.

Boston on Guns & Courage
5½"x8½", 192 pages. Published March 1998.
Prices each: *1-5* copies are Ø17; *6-31* copies are Ø10.20; *32-59* copies are Ø9.50; a case of *64* or more copies are Ø8.50 each.

Boston on Surviving Y2K
5½"x8½", 352 pages. Published November 1998.
Prices each: *1-5* copies are Ø22; *6-15* copies are Ø13.20; *16-35* copies are Ø12.30; a case of *36* or more copies are Ø11 each.

Shipping and Handling are *not* included. Book Rate add: Ø3 for first copy and Ø0.25 per additional copy. First Class add: Ø4 and Ø0.50.

These forms of payment *only:*
Cash (Preferred. Cash orders get autographed copies.)
payee blank M.O.s (Which makes them more easily negotiable.)
credit cards (Many of our distributors take them. See our website.)

Unless prior agreement has been made, we do not accept (*and will return*) checks, C.O.D.s, filled-in M.O.s, or any other form of tender. Prices and terms are subject to change without notice (check our website first). Send orders to:

JAVELIN PRESS
c/o P.O. Box 31B; Ignacio, Colorado. (81137-0031)
www.javelinpress.com